Introduction
From Socialite to Satrap

'Oh! I have got a problem,' Naveen Patnaik burst out spontaneously, before quickly falling quiet on a balmy evening in the spring of 2000.

The 53-year-old Naveen was on the cusp of taking over as the chief minister of Odisha (then spelt as 'Orissa'). He was set to embark on an incredible journey that would see him becoming one of the country's longest-serving chief ministers, second only to Sikkim's Pawan Kumar Chamling.

Over the next quarter of a century, Naveen set new records, getting re-elected again and again – no less than five times in total.

Given his durability at the very top of his state despite the unpredictability that invariably comes along with any electoral democracy where elected leaders fall by the wayside routinely, the secret of

Naveen's spectacular success has long been the subject of a mystery as gripping as any Agatha Christie thriller. What allowed him to tick along for so long – some 24 years at Odisha's helm – has been the subject of never-ending debates amongst people interested in Indian politics.

His exclamation – 'Oh! I have got a problem' – while being driven around in a car from one television studio to another for in-person interviews in Bhubaneswar (the capital city of Odisha) – was out of character. Taciturn by nature, Naveen rarely spoke. When he did, he spoke softly and cautiously. His car pulled into a TV studio soon after he made that comment.

It was the day that the 2000-assembly election results were being announced and he was headed for a thumping victory. It was clear that he would be sworn in as the next chief minister, but Naveen surprisingly had no security accompanying him. I was with him in a rented car. He sat in front, beside the driver; I was in the back. Those were the pre-EVM days – the counting of ballots was still underway and the results of several seats were awaited. In some cases, trends were known, but official announcements of who had won and who had lost were yet to be made.

As results were confirmed and friends called on my mobile, I relayed them to Naveen. 'X has won from

Naveen Patnaik

Naveen Patnaik

Ruben Banerjee

juggernaut

JUGGERNAUT BOOKS
C-I-128, First Floor, Sangam Vihar, Near Holi Chowk,
New Delhi 110080, India

First published in hardback by Juggernaut Books 2018
Published in paperback by Juggernaut Books 2024

10 9 8 7 6 5 4 3 2

P-ISBN: 9789353453169
E-ISBN: 9789353456887

Typeset in Adobe Caslon Pro by R. Ajith Kumar, New Delhi

Printed at Thomson Press India Ltd

To my late father, Tara Pada Banerjee
Baba, I know you would have been very proud

Contents

Contents

here, Y has lost from there' – I kept updating him. Naveen merely listened, poker-faced. He soaked in whatever information I offered him. But then came the result from Pallahara, an assembly constituency in the central Anugul district, and Naveen's ears pricked up. Naveen's new party, the Biju Janata Dal (BJD), had contested the elections in alliance with the Bharatiya Janata Party (BJP), and the winning candidate from Pallahara happened to be the BJP's Dharmendra Pradhan. The moment I broke the news that Pradhan had won, Naveen said, 'Oh! I have got a problem'.

Son of the then union minister of state for surface transport, Debendra Pradhan, Dharmendra was a little-known figure in 2000. An activist of the BJP's student wing, the Akhil Bharatiya Vidyarthi Parishad (ABVP), and a former student union leader of Utkal University, Dharmendra was contesting elections for the first time. Nobody thought much of him and many in the state BJP felt he would, at best, be a temporary presence. Odisha, like every other state, was replete with instances of leaders fading into oblivion after winning one or two elections, and the consensus was that Dharmendra would be no different.

But clearly, Naveen thought differently and blurted out his concern over Dharmendra's victory in a rare moment of candour.

Why he felt that way is what makes Naveen truly intriguing. That a first-time MLA's election was clocked, with alarm, by Naveen way back in 2000 – when merely a few in the state took Dharmendra seriously – puts him in an entirely different league of politicians. It also possibly holds the key to understanding what made Naveen such a successful politician. He had this innate power to gauge any opponent's potential power well in advance, and Dharmendra – now an influential union minister – had set alarm bells ringing in him since the beginning.

A top IAS officer who had served Naveen for a long time insisted that Naveen possessed 'X-ray eyes'. He was suspicious by nature. The moment he saw a person, he sized them up, without letting the person know what he was thinking of them. 'Naveen's gut feelings were strong and he relied heavily on them,' another senior official explained. Those who have worked with him closely say that Naveen could hide his emotions well. He may have had a very poor opinion of someone, but the person would never get to know that. On the contrary, it was more likely that Naveen would floor them with his warmth and charm.

This happened with Dharmendra as well. A few days after his private remark, Naveen met Dharmendra in the assembly when the new house convened to welcome the newly elected legislators. Naveen, who was the chief minister by then, congratulated the first-time BJP MLA profusely and said how happy he was seeing Dharmendra win. Naveen, after all, could never be faulted for failing to show courtesy in public.

Precisely 24 years later, Naveen's premonition about his problem proved prophetic. Dharmendra – the 'problem' – settled down at his home in Bhubaneswar's Prachi Enclave to watch disaster unfold for Naveen on a giant television screen. It was the morning of 4 June 2024, when the votes for the 2024 general elections and the Odisha state assembly polls were being counted. In the intervening years, Naveen and his 'problem' had chartered different courses. Naveen kept winning election after election in the state and seemed virtually invincible. Dharmendra, too, had grown in heft, having graduated from a rookie legislator to the union minister of education.

Comforted by his visits to two places of worship – the Chausathi Yogini temple in Hirapur the previous night and the Maa Ugratara temple in Khordha in the morning – Dharmendra patiently awaited the results of the elections held simultaneously for the state's 21 Lok Sabha and 147 assembly seats. Besides being a frontline leader of the BJP who had contributed his might to queer the pitch for Naveen, Dharmendra himself was in the fray for a parliamentary seat from Sambalpur in western Odisha. As the results trickled in, cagey nervousness gave way to cautious optimism, and eventually, to unbridled excitement. The unthinkable had happened: Naveen's BJD had been defeated and the BJP had been voted into power for the first time in the state. In the polls for the parliamentary seats, the BJD had drawn an embarrassing blank.

A few days later, it was the turn of Dharmendra to be at his courteous best as he and other BJP bigwigs – Prime Minister Narendra Modi included – went the extra mile to welcome the outgoing chief minister to the dais for the oath-taking ceremony of the new chief minister. It was a fine show of electoral democracy at its decent best.

Though reduced to being just a *former* chief minister, the aura around Naveen remains undiminished. He still invokes as much awe among people as he did during his heyday. Now 78-years-old, he also commands the grudging respect of opponents as a politically astute patriarch.

Reticent, reclusive and refined, Naveen has been a surprise package in the crass and chaotic world of politics. The youngest son of the legendary politician Biju Patnaik, he has blue-blooded pedigree and a powerful surname. Yet, initially, only a few thought much of him and almost certainly never imagined that he would reach the dizzying heights that he ultimately scaled.

I, too, was one of them when I first ran into him in 1988 at Konark, the seaside resort with the famous Sun temple, not far from the more famous temple town of Puri. A British explorer and writer, Mark Shand – brother of Queen Camilla – was set to embark on a thousand-odd-kilometre journey from Konark to Sonepur (in the neighbouring Bihar) on an elephant, creating a buzz and drawing a motley crowd. Invited as a guest of the private secretary of Biju Patnaik – Naveen's famous father and then the leader of the opposition in the Odisha legislature – I was loitering around in the lawns of the Konark inspection bungalow when Gour Mohan Sarangi, the private secretary, introduced me to a tall, lean, middle-aged man in jeans and T-shirt walking by.

'Hi, I am Naveen,' said the man, extending his hand for a warm handshake.

That was that, and we all moved towards Mark Shand as the adventurer arrived with his entourage a trifle late. I cannot be faulted for taking the fortuitous meeting lightly. Biju Babu's family generally stayed in the background, away from the public gaze. Occasionally, his wife, Gyan Patnaik, would make an appearance beside the imposing, six feet-plus-tall politician, who left a deep imprint on the state, both during his life and after. But more often than not, Gyan Patnaik, when seen in public, would only be a silent spectator, while Biju Babu held court. His children were rarely seen.

Biju Babu's children – eldest child Prem, daughter Gita, and Naveen – lived mostly outside Odisha. Naveen lived in his father's privately owned New Delhi residence on Aurangzeb Road, now known as the A.P.J. Abdul Kalam Marg. They visited their father in Bhubaneswar from time to time, but the family visits were invariably low-key.

Since Biju Babu's children only had a peripheral role, no one at Konark showed any interest in Naveen. No one crowded around him or sought to grab his attention. To his credit, Naveen kept to himself and threw none of the tantrums associated with children of the famous and the powerful. At that time, no one in Odisha or elsewhere could have dreamt that Biju Babu's younger son was destined to outshine his illustrious father.

But almost a decade after Shand undertook his epic elephant journey, those of us who had been somewhat dismissive of Naveen in Konark were forced to take note of him. I, for one, had the onerous task of chasing him for news reports. A political nonentity, Naveen was catapulted into the limelight following his father's death in 1997. Circumstances forced him to plunge into politics, and over time, he outshone his distinguished father. Consider this: for all his fame,

Biju Babu had only short stints in power. His political career spanned some fifty years, but the legendary leader was in power for less than ten years in total. He was the chief minister of Odisha for about two years in the early 1960s. After spending a long spell in the wilderness thereafter, he next tasted power in the late 1970s, when a disparate opposition under Jayaprakash Narayan ousted Indira Gandhi from the Centre. Biju Babu was the union minister of steel and mines in the Janata government for a little over two years until the government fell. Biju Babu himself continued to be a powerful regional player, but held no executive post until 1990, when he again became chief minister. He remained in office until the completion of his term in 1995.

But unlike his father's roller-coaster ride, Naveen's political journey mostly had an upward trajectory till 2024. After his father's death, Naveen quickly became a member of Parliament (MP) after winning the Lok Sabha by-election to Aska constituency in 1997 – the seat his father had won in 1996 – and then got re-elected to Parliament twice in quick succession, first in March 1998 and then again in October 1999. When the National Democratic Alliance (NDA) led by Prime Minister Atal Bihari Vajpayee came to power in 1998, Naveen became a union minister. He remained a union minister when Vajpayee took oath as prime minister again the following year. He then set his sights on Odisha and when elections were held in the state in 2000, he swept the polls and became the chief minister.

He stayed on as the chief minister until he was ousted in 2024.

In the 24 years he held office, the world changed a lot. Naveen came to power in an era before the 9/11 and the 2008 financial crisis. India, too, changed considerably. The NDA led by the BJP was voted out in 2004 and replaced by the United Progressive Alliance (UPA), which had the grand old Congress party at its helm. It lorded over the country for ten years until a groundswell of popular disenchantment swept it aside and propelled Narendra Modi to the top job of prime minister in 2014.

On the economic front as well, there have been sea changes. To give just one example, the Sensex which hovered around 4,000 in the year 2000 – the year Naveen first assumed charge as Odisha's chief minister – is now trading above 75,000 and shows an upward bias.

Odisha, however, showed little political upheaval until very recently, when the 2024 elections finally ended Naveen's uninterrupted long run. Unlike many other chief ministers who were felled by anti-incumbency after winning landslide victories in their states, Naveen largely bucked the trend. Even in 2014, when the Modi phenomenon swept across the length and breadth of the country, it made no dent in Odisha. In fact, Naveen improved on the previous tally of the BJD in the assembly elections. In the Lok Sabha, the BJD won twenty of the twenty-one seats in the state.

All this and more made Naveen a remarkable phenomenon. Unlike other politicians with a penchant for being in the headlines, he was rarely seen on prime-time television, and heard even less. He could qualify as the quietest politician in present-day India. Back home in Odisha, there was an information deficit about Naveen. People knew the basic details of his social life before he entered politics in 1997, courtesy some of his journalist friends, but little else.

That Naveen, together with some of his friends, ran a boutique – *Psychedelhi* – in the capital's Oberoi hotel once was little-known. The boutique's clientele included famous persons such as The Beatles. The people of Odisha knew he was some sort of a writer before, but generally had no idea of how many and what kinds of books he had written. Few had seen or read the three coffee table books Biju Babu's son had authored – *A Second Paradise: Indian Courtly Life 1590-1947*, *A Desert Kingdom: The Rajputs of Bikaner* and *The Garden of Life: An Introduction to the Healing Plants of India*. Even fewer people knew that Naveen had acted in a bit role in a 1988 Ivory Merchant film, *The Deceivers*, which had established actors such as Pierce Brosnan, Shashi Kapoor and Saeed Jaffrey in the cast.

Journalist Tavleen Singh's book *Durbar* is replete with references to a younger Naveen who went party-hopping with her and was a permanent feature of Delhi's cocktail circuit. Singh recounts an episode when a young Naveen asked Sonia Gandhi at a party if she was wearing clothes made by Valentino, the Italian couturier. Renowned editor-journalist Vir Sanghvi, in an article published several years ago, wrote on Naveen's lifestyle and the reputation he had as the perfect host. Naveen's Delhi home, Sanghvi wrote, was a cultural melting pot, where the high and mighty, the rich and famous – and the not-so-famous – gathered routinely. Among his guests were Mick Jagger of the Rolling Stones, actress Koo Stark, who once dated Prince Andrew of Britain, and Bruce Chatwin, the famous travel writer and novelist.

Though Naveen lived mostly away from the public gaze, his social contacts were legendary. One time, one of Naveen's foreign acquaintances apparently called up to ask if he could host a friend who would pass through India shortly. Naveen said yes and the person, who was identified only as Robert, came and stayed with him for a few days. It was none other than the Hollywood superstar Robert De Niro.

Such stories, combined with Naveen's reticence, gave him an aura of mystery. People seemed to like him but knew precious little about him. There is practically no one who knows him intimately, at least not in Odisha, prompting some to compare him with Greta Garbo, the Swedish-born American actress whose mystique deepened after she became a recluse on retirement.

There is only one other politician in India who had been chief minister longer than Naveen. Pawan Kumar Chamling, who was chief minister of Sikkim between 1994 and 2019, and hence ruled for 24 years and 165 days. Naveen had occupied the chief minister's chair for 24 years and 99 days – nearly a year longer than the third-place record holder: West Bengal's Jyoti Basu, who had ruled for a little over 23 years.

But it isn't only his longevity that has leapfrogged Naveen to the status of a living legend. Politics, by and large, is a sordid, murky and fiercely competitive affair. It is a treacherous vocation where everyone is out to pull one and all down by any means, fair or foul. The world of politics in Odisha is no different: it was, in fact, the first state in the country where an elected people's representative switched political allegiances after winning at the polls. Bira Kishore Behera had changed sides and joined the Independent Party of a local maharaja after being elected on a Congress ticket from Jajpur district in the provincial elections during British times, in 1937, thereby setting into motion a practice that came to later be decried as the politics of '*Aaya Ram, gaya Ram* (Ram has come, Ram has left)'.

Surviving such a cut-throat political set-up is no easy task. Naveen was a political novice in 1997, with little to no knowledge of the state. His pedigree and powerful surname did give him a head start, but to sustain the momentum for more than two decades, consolidating his hold on the state, going from strength to strength, was no mean achievement. From a greenhorn, Naveen smoothly transitioned into a regional satrap.

Remarkably, when he first took over as chief minister, he spoke no Odia. Rally after rally, ahead of the 2000 assembly elections, a somewhat sheepish Naveen went around telling the crowds that he would take time to pick up the local language – '*Mote bhala Odia kahiba paeen tike samay lagiba*' – before switching over to reading from a pre-written speech in Hindi. Imagine Mamata Banerjee seeking to become chief minister of Bengal without speaking Bengali, or Nitish Kumar becoming chief minister of Bihar without knowing a word of Bhojpuri. Or for that matter, Narendra Modi hoping to lead Gujarat, as he did for over twelve years before becoming prime minister, without knowing Gujarati.

Twenty-four years later, when he has finally stepped down, it cannot be said Naveen's Odia has vastly improved. He is more at ease speaking in English than the language of the state that he represented for so long. The jury is also out on whether Naveen delivered on the hope he gave people and lived up to their expectations. For all the publicity and propaganda that his successive governments undertook aggressively, Odisha still makes news for the wrong reasons. Children in the state's outlying areas are malnourished, poverty is rampant, and corruption, critics say, is endemic. Despite the long years of Naveen at the helm, Odisha's enduring image is that of a state neck-deep in despair and distress. Naveen gave the state stability, but his opponents say he failed miserably in bringing succour to the people.

But irrespective of his achievements or failings, it cannot be denied that Naveen scripted a spectacular success story for himself. Having had nothing to do with politics for approximately the first fifty years of his life, he transformed himself into a consummate politician once he decided to take the plunge. Some say Naveen had politics in his genes even though this instinct had lain dormant for decades. When the opportunity finally presented itself after his father's demise, he simply outdid others with a mix of shrewdness and stealth – qualities that he inherently possessed. But he also owed a part of his political success to the state's disappointing political past. For decades before his arrival, the state seemed adrift on hopelessness. Politicians played their inane games ceaselessly and scandals erupted at regular intervals. When Naveen stepped forward to stake claim to his father's legacy, the Odias, wallowing in misery, responded wholeheartedly. It was as if the quest for collective redemption, an attempt to retrieve trust, integrity and morality that were in short supply in public life, had begun in right earnest with Naveen's arrival.

~

I had a taste of the muck that dominated Odisha's politics within hours of my arrival in the state for the first time, way back in 1987, when the paan-chewing man with stained teeth, sitting behind the small desk at the chief minister's official residence, said, 'Asila? Asa.'

Less than ten-hours-old in Bhubaneswar, I was stumped by the words. I struggled to make sense of what the slightly balding man was saying. Or *why* he was saying it.

The words in Odia seemed somewhat similar to my mother tongue, Bengali: 'So have you have? Come.' The man seemed to have been expecting me and was welcoming me inside. Obviously, he had mistaken me for someone else. But before I could fully comprehend what he had said, he spoke up again. '*Ratri egaratare asiba* (Come at eleven at night),' he said, this time with a suggestive half-smile.

Since my arrival that morning as the state correspondent of *The Indian Express*, I had been caught up in a virtual whirlwind. Bhubaneswar those days was known for a cool breeze that invariably blew across the leafy, tree-lined city, but the political temperatures had been rising and the city was divided, with battle lines drawn between loyalists of the chief minister J.B. Patnaik (not related to Biju Babu or Naveen in any way) and his rivals.

J.B. Patnaik's detractors within the ruling Congress were demanding his dismissal and I arrived just when yet another bout of dissidence was threatening to unseat the normally unflappable chief minister. Disgust at the political classes, including the chief minister, was at an all-time high in the aftermath of a damning cover story that the now-defunct *Illustrated Weekly of India* had run in May 1986 on the alleged sexual escapades of J.B. Patnaik.

The story portrayed J.B. Patnaik as a modern-day Caligula, the notorious Roman emperor known for his mood swings and testosterone-driven orgies. The *Illustrated Weekly* quoted men and women giving details of Patnaik's sexual preferences and how they had been enticed to be at his service. The chief minister was shown to be a 'deviant'. The levelled allegations were serious, but far from conclusive. J.B. Patnaik doggedly denied the charges and took the magazine to court. Unable (or unwilling) to back up the allegations, the *Illustrated Weekly* was forced to apologize. But by then, the damage had been done and the chief minister's image and standing had been severely dented. Party rivals wanted him dismissed and senior Congress leader Uma Shankar Dixit was at Bhubaneswar to mediate between the warring pro- and anti-J.B. Patnaik factions.

Soon after he touched down, Dixit left for Raj Bhavan and the journalists assembled at the airport decided to head to J.B. Patnaik's official residence. I followed them and was puzzled by the light – almost absent – security at the chief minister's house. The journalists marched ahead, first past a portico and then through a small anteroom. By the time I got into the anteroom, the other journalists had moved into the next room – presumably where J.B. Patnaik was. So, there I was, standing alone in front of the desk and the paan-chewing man behind it. He did not know I was a journalist and said, *'Asila? Asa. Ratri egaratare asiba'*. As I stood there, unsure, a journalist came back and pulled me inside, sparing me further embarrassment.

Nearly four decades later, I am yet to decode the real meaning of the words spoken by the man. Was it an innocuous welcome? Or was it an invitation of the kind that the *Illustrated Weekly* report had famously hinted were frequently given out?

~

Whatever it was, it got me hooked to Odisha from day one. My fascination grew overtime, with every twist and turn the state took in the following years, sprinkled liberally with murders, mayhem and mass misery. Events that unfolded in Odisha were mostly tragic, but at times, the changing situations also provided for some comic relief. In December 1989, when J.B. Patnaik finally made way for a change of guard in the state, his successor, Hemananda Biswal, was woken up from his sleep by a party emissary in the cold winter night, to be told that he would become chief minister the next day. Those were pre-cellphone times and Biswal's only landline at home, given to him as a member of the Legislative Assembly (MLA), had been disconnected by the service provider for non-payment of dues. Biswal was stunned by the sudden good tidings. The emissary, the son of a former Congress chief minister, was stumped by Biswal's over-the-top reaction. '*Ha ha ha, mu mukhamantri hebi!* (Ha ha ha, I will become the chief minister!)', a surprised Biswal kept repeating aloud, as he paced up and down the lawns of his house, soaking in the news that night. First elected an MLA in 1974, Biswal, from the western district of Sundargarh, was a veteran politician, and commanded respect within the party. But the Congress, as always, was faction-ridden, and Biswal was not in the race to become chief minister until the party high command, prodded by the new state Congress chief, Nandini Satpathy, decided to crown him. By making him chief minister, Satpathy expected to be the real power behind the throne. Biswal, nonetheless, was overjoyed. He laughed more the next day, when the same service provider installed no less than seven landlines at his home after he had taken oath as the new chief minister.

Not short of either drama or melodrama, Odisha never ceased to surprise and shock. In December 1999, the Congress wanted to sack its chief minister, Giridhar Gamang, for his bumbling ways. A delegation of top leaders arrived to hand him his pink slip, but Gamang refused to go easily. He kept hopping from place to place across the city, with the leaders in hot pursuit. He escaped them and flew off to Delhi, where other senior Congress leaders finally cornered him and extracted his resignation.

Naveen, on the contrary, was his own master – he had no high command peering over his shoulder – and he brought stability to the topsy-turvy world of Odisha politics. But his reign did not rob the state of either the drama or the intrigue that was intrinsic to the way its politics was conducted. High-voltage action was never in short supply as the new chief minister stamped his authority by cutting down to size rivals he thought could sabotage him later. As Naveen grew in stature, most of his erstwhile comrades were made to bite the dust. Plots were hatched and daggers were drawn periodically, and Naveen gave repeated proof that he was no pushover.

The key to Naveen's success was that even though he indulged in political machinations and subterfuge, he largely came out without any blemishes, skillfully sidestepping scrutiny and deflecting criticism. He continued to be viewed by many as innocent and incapable of the maneuvering of an ordinary politician. And when something went horribly wrong somewhere in the state, there was always someone else to shoulder the blame, sparing Naveen any taint.

That he was single, soft-spoken and always deferential, helped in nurturing Naveen's image. It may have frayed at the edges after his very long

stint in power, but a sizeable section of the people
still believes that he had no reason to be corrupt
as he had no children to pass his wealth to. Many
others refuse to associate anything nasty with the
unfailingly pleasant and gentle Naveen. All this and
more made his journey – from a socialite at ease in
the rarefied cocktail circuit of Delhi to a regional
czar astonishingly adept in the tumultuous world of
politics – truly remarkable.

1

Mere Pitaji Ko . . . Bahut Pyara Tha

The twin-engine helicopter flew low, skirting over swathes of hills, valleys and fields. Having taken off from Bhubaneswar, the chopper was headed towards Thakurmunda, a speck of a town in the state's interiors.

From that height, the ground below looked picturesque. Plantations stretched mile upon mile, punctuated occasionally by rivers that cut across the terrain before vanishing into the horizon in a serpentine maze. Rolling hills gave way to small valleys, which in turn made space for another range of hills. Hamlets peeped out intermittently, the tin and thatched roofs of ordinary huts belonging to dirt-poor families glinting charmingly under the bright sun. Narrow pathways etched magical designs on the landscape, and brimming village ponds encircled by trees and the cattle wandering about gave the impression of uninterrupted bliss.

Nothing from the top betrayed the turmoil that the people of Odisha – which accounted for 4.8 per cent of the country's land mass and 3.47 per cent of its population – had endured in recent months. A killer cyclone had ploughed through the state in October 1999, leaving 10,000 people dead and destroying everything in its wake.

From the time it was carved out as a province in 1936, Odisha has been among the poorest Indian states. Though the state is culturally rich – home to temples, textiles, breathtaking tourist spots such as the mangroves of Bhitarkanika and the classical dance form Odissi – it barely caught the attention of the rest of the country except fleetingly when the media reported on the chronic hunger and starvation there or on a natural disaster as big as the supercyclone.

As the helicopter flew overhead that day in the year 2000, the situation below was the bleakest it had been in living memory, second it would seem only to the 1866 'Na Anka' famine, which had wiped out a third of its population. Nature's wrath, combined with administrative bungling of no lesser magnitude, had crippled the state and its people. In the weeks following the cyclone, the state's politicians bickered shamelessly and held the administration hostage. While the incumbent Congress chief minister bumbled about, his senior party colleagues rushed to New Delhi to petition the party leadership to have him replaced, taking advantage of the chaos to push their personal agendas and chief ministerial ambitions. Relief did not reach the survivors in time and hundreds of thousands went hungry as the state administration struggled to cope with the scale of the disaster. The government abdicated its responsibility and as good as abandoned its subjects. Politicking took centre stage and the people, left to fend for themselves, were looking heavenwards for divine help when the helicopter made its low-key entry from the distant horizon.

In the helicopter, a fifty-something man, of a tall, lean frame, sat silently in the front seat, beside the pilot. But for the routine pleasantries at the start of the journey, few words were spoken. The man, in a starched white kurta-pyjama, occasionally stretched his legs, perhaps silenced by the daunting challenge ahead of him.

Naveen Patnaik had reasons to be in a contemplative mood. He was a rank outsider who had lived most of his adult life outside Odisha, spoke no Odia and was, for good measure, a stranger to its history, culture, traditions, rituals and everything else. Yet he was on the campaign trail, hoping to become the chief minister of a state hit with the worst tragedy in recent times.

Educated at Doon School and a classmate of Sanjay Gandhi's, he was more at home speaking in English with a western accent. He loved Dunhill cigarettes and enjoyed his Famous Grouse whiskey every evening, a habit that he struggled to give up even in his advanced years. Right until he took the plunge into politics, Naveen had been a permanent fixture in Delhi's most exclusive party circuits and rubbed shoulders routinely with the well-heeled and powerful. He had, in his younger days, run a boutique called Psychedelhi from the premises of the Oberoi hotel and his clientele included the fabled Beatles. His circle of friends straddled the globe and his interests included books and films, landing him a small role in Merchant Ivory's 1988 adventure film *The Deceivers*, which had Pierce Brosnan and Saeed Jaffrey in the cast.

In 1997, one thing led to another in quick succession and Naveen shed his jeans and T-shirt for the politician's preferred attire – kurta-pyjama – to tap into the outpouring of goodwill for his recently deceased father, Biju Patnaik. Barely months after his father died, he contested the by-election from Aksa, the seat his father represented at the time of his death, on a Janata Dal ticket, the party his late father belonged to, and won handsomely. 'I have inherited my father's responsibilities, but no privileges,' Naveen famously told the *India Today* magazine shortly after taking the electoral plunge. 'One of the members of his [Biju Babu's] family had to continue his legacy of social responsibility,' he said.

By December 1997 he had founded a regional outfit called the Biju Janata Dal and was re-elected as an MP in 1998 and 1999 as the country held general elections in quick succession amid political instability. But by the time Atal Bihari Vajpayee was sworn in as the head of the BJP-led NDA government in 1998, Naveen had become a BJP ally and Vajpayee rewarded him by making him the union minister for steel and mines.

When Naveen entered politics in Odisha, he was trying to reach out to the people of his native land whose rusticity he did not share. Yet, as the son of Odisha's legendary politician, he had been anointed by fate and destiny as the desperate state's only possible saviour. Fed up with the games played by discredited politicians, many Odias welcomed Naveen despite his lack of Odia. They knew little about him other than that he was Biju Babu's son. But the anonymity of his past meant a freedom from being judged. At a time when almost the entire political class was steeped in infamy, Naveen appeared to be refreshingly innocent, a breath of fresh air in a putrid environment. In more ways than one, Naveen was the Arvind Kejriwal of his time, the clean political outsider who had come to perform surgery on a malignant polity. Just as Kejriwal, the Aam Aadmi Party leader, caught the imagination of Delhi in 2015 and swept almost everyone off their feet, Naveen had Odias swooning over him.

Take for instance the rally Naveen attended early in his political career at Panikoili, which is on the national highway running through Bhubaneswar and the coastal town of Balasore further north, a must-stop for long-distance commuters en route to Kolkata for steaming hot meals at its famed dhabas. The Janata Dal hosted an anti-Congress rally in the town and Naveen came to make a speech as the party's newly elected MP.

In attendance were senior Janata Dal leaders such as Srikanta Jena, once a close aide of Biju Babu's, who had risen to become the union parliamentary affairs minister in the I.K. Gujral government in New Delhi. Jena nursed ambitions for himself in the post-Biju era and hoped to make his mark at the first major rally aimed at uniting the anti-Congress forces in the state. But the moment he began his speech, slippers and shoes of various shapes and sizes began raining down on the stage.

A career politician, Jena kept his composure and continued with his speech. But the crowd was becoming aggressive and the other leaders on the stage began getting jittery. They kept tugging at

Jena's kurta from behind, prodding him to wrap up his speech quickly. The mike was then handed over to Naveen. Naveen rose from his chair, walked towards the dais and waved at the crowd. The jeers turned into lusty cheers almost immediately: It was the first indicator that Naveen had a readymade connect with the people.

Some three years later, on his way to Thakurmunda on board the helicopter, Naveen knew he was more popular than ever. The killer cyclone had scooped up the sea and brought it some twenty-two kilometres inland at its raging peak in 1999. Now after the waters had receded, another wave rose high: this time for Naveen.

As the town showed up in the distance, Naveen reached into his kurta pocket and pulled out a neatly folded paper that his assistant had given him. On it was written, in bold, the word 'Thakurmunda' in English. Naveen kept reading the name over and over again until he had memorized it.

The presence of outsiders – politicians and journalists – in the town that hit national and international headlines in 1999 for the gruesome killing in its vicinity of an Australian missionary and his two sons by the Hindu zealot Dara Singh as the three victims slept in a car, had brought out the residents in droves. A mass of men, women and children waved their arms frantically in unbridled enthusiasm as the 'famous son' whom many saw as their one last hope stepped out from the storm of dust kicked up by the helicopter.

Naveen did not disappoint. He strode to the stage prepared for him and took over the microphone.

'*Mere pitaji ko Thakurmunda bahut pyara tha*' (My father loved Thakurmunda very much) he said softly into the microphone after the perfunctory namaskar. Naveen spoke in his gruff voice, but its effect was electrifying. The residents of Thakurmunda were ecstatic that Biju Babu had told his son about their town in the back of beyond. Whoops of collective joy erupted and the rally site resonated with chants of 'Naveen Patnaik zindabad'.

Another rehearsed line followed: '*Mere pitaji ne bola tha beta Thakurmunda zaroor jana.*' (My father had said, 'Son, you must definitely go to Thakurmunda.') The crowds were delirious with joy that the place of their birth was so dear to Biju Babu – even if his son addressed them in Hindi.

Naveen did not have to continue much longer beyond that. He already had the locals under his spell. He touched briefly on some of the things he would do – part of his poll promises – before wrapping up his speech with a namaste and another round of deft hand-waving at the crowd. He then boarded the helicopter which was to transport him to the second rally planned for the day, at Kendrapara.

The same routine was repeated. As the outskirts of the town came into view, Naveen again reached into his pocket and another piece of paper emerged, this time with the name 'Kendrapara' written in bold. He read it again and again as he readied to take the prominent coastal town by storm.

'*Mere pitaji ko Kendrapara bahut pyara tha,*' Naveen said when his turn came to address the rally. The effect of the words was the same as in Thakurmunda. The crowds turned ecstatic.

When the claimant to the chief minister's chair presented his second line, '*Mere pitaji ne bola tha beta Kendrapara zaroor jana,*' the crowd went berserk and the police struggled to control the sea of humanity crushing against the barricades.

The job done, Naveen took off for Satyabadi, a town in Puri district with special significance for Odia pride. Gopabandhu Das, the state's best-known freedom fighter, fondly remembered as 'Utkalmani' (jewel of Utkal), had lived and worked here, making the town a popular place of pilgrimage.

Listening to Naveen narrate what his father had told him, Satyabadi replacing Thakurmunda and Kendrapara, the locals felt more pride welling inside them. Their response was much the same as at the earlier two stopovers. Biju Babu's heir had them virtually eating out of his hand.

It was the kind of rapturous response that politicians would die for. But Naveen had it all fall into his lap. He swept the state effortlessly. Other sons of famous parents have had similar head starts, former prime minister Rajiv Gandhi included, but few had such intense love and affection bestowed on them so unquestioningly.

Odisha, in fact, has never been short of famous sons and many of them are still in public life. Former chief minister Harekrushna Mahtab's son Bhartruhari is an MP from Cuttack. A.U. Singh Deo, the son of another ex-chief minister, R.N. Singh Deo, was alternately a minister in the state and an MP for over two decades. A.U. Singh Deo's mantle has been passed on to his articulate son Kalikesh, who once got elected as the MP from Balangir before being elected an MLA. Also in the crowded arena of famous sons is Tathagatha Satpathy, the son of former chief minister Nandini Satpathy. Tathagatha was the MP from Dhenkanal – his mother's bastion – for several terms until he voluntarily abstained from electoral politics.

Like Naveen, the other children had famous surnames and commanded instant recognition. But the similarities ended there. No one was accorded the kind of ecstatic reception that was rolled out for

Biju Babu's heir. For one, the legacies the other scions inherited were limited and lacked statewide mass appeal. A former royal, R.N. Singh Deo had a high stature, but his political influence after his death was confined to the territory that his family once ruled – Balangir. In her lifetime, Nandini Satpathy was viewed as the Odisha version of Indira Gandhi and revered as the Iron Lady. But once past her political prime, her appeal was restricted largely to her home district of Dhenkanal.

But for the head starts they got in terms of securing party tickets to contest elections the first time, the other sons have had to struggle to stay afloat in the cut-throat world of politics. They have won elections and also lost elections. A.U. Singh Deo has lost several elections as has Tathagatha. Bhartruhari is an MP from the old city of Cuttack, but his influence is virtually non-existent beyond the borders of his parliamentary constituency.

But being Biju Patnaik's son was different. Like everyone else, Biju Babu, in his long political career, had won and lost elections aplenty. In 1971, a particular bad year for him, he contested five elections – one Lok Sabha and four assembly seats – and lost all of them. Yet, he was like no other politician.

Imperious, influential and hugely charismatic, Biju Babu claimed a space for himself in Odia folklore.

As a young man, he was a pilot, employed with the Indian National Airways. At the start of the Second World War, he joined the Royal Indian Air Force. He routinely undertook dangerous missions, including flying from Baku, Azerbaijan, to airdrop arms to the Russian Red Army besieged by the Germans in Stalingrad. He also dodged bombing and strafing in early 1942 to evacuate British officials and civilians from Burma, occupied by the Japanese.

India's first prime minister, Jawaharlal Nehru, turned to him in 1947 to rescue Indonesian resistance fighters under attack from Dutch colonizers. With Gyan Patnaik, his wife, who was also a trained pilot, beside him, Biju Babu flew a Dakota and dodged bullets from the ground to fly out several prominent nationalist leaders, including Prime Minister Sutan Sjahrir, to safety. Indonesian President Sukarno conferred the title of 'Bhumiputra' or 'The Son of the Soil' on him and gave him honorary citizenship. In India his bravery got him fawning fans and a larger-than-life stature.

Biju Babu also negotiated the treacherous territory of business, setting up an industrial empire in the mid 1940s. He founded the Orissa Textile Mills in 1946 and the business prospered in no time, employing 5000 people within five years. The mill had 48,000 spindles and 864 looms, producing a variety of garments from saris to dhotis. Around the same time, he also started his own Kalinga Airlines, which was later merged with Indian Airlines when the national carrier came into being in the early 1950s. In between, he set up a tube mill and a refrigerator factory. But never a conformist nor conventional, he gradually gave up his businesses and focused, instead, on politics.

His bravado was exemplary and his temper legendary. As his novelist daughter Gita Mehta was to write later, Biju Babu was once flying a British officer from a remote desert post in western India when he heard the officer talking disparagingly about his flying skills. Biju Babu landed the plane on a desolate stretch and told the Britisher he could walk back!

Over time, Biju Babu came to represent the aspirations of an average Odia. Courageous and adventurous, he knew everybody who mattered in the country. What he said mattered. People lovingly called him the 'Kalinga Shandha' (Odisha Bull). Biju Babu upheld that image with his regular bluster.

Modesty wasn't his strength and he routinely voiced views that bordered on political incorrectness. For example, when an animated discussion at his office veered round to corruption in public life and his party, he commented, 'What is honesty? Honesty is nothing but a lack of opportunity.'

During his political career, Biju Babu flirted with various political parties and once even floated his own. He began as a Congressman and had the ear of Prime Minister Nehru. As mentioned earlier, he served as chief minister of Odisha for two years in the early 1960s. But once Indira Gandhi took over as the undisputed leader of the Congress, Biju Babu's stock plummeted. He was forced to break away from the Congress and float his own outfit, the Utkal Congress, in 1970. For a while he was part of Charan Singh's Bharatiya Lok Dal, which was formed following the merger of the Utkal Congress and six other political parties, to oppose Indira Gandhi. In 1977, post-Emergency, a disparate opposition came together to float the Janata Party and Biju Babu featured prominently in it. Biju Babu served as minister for steel and mines for two years in the Janata government. In the latter half of the 1980s, when the opposition came together against Rajiv Gandhi and the Janata Dal was formed, Biju Babu was once again at the forefront of the formation. He remained with the Janata Dal till his very end.

Biju Babu loved taking risks and ploughed his personal wealth into financing his politics. He spent long years out of power and faced near-total bankruptcy. 'He is one politician whose wealth diminished after decades in politics,' recollected an old associate.

But Brand Biju survived all the tumult and towards the end of his long career came another chance to storm back into power. Biju Babu seized the opportunity in his inimitable style. By the late 1980s, it was quite apparent that the nation was rooting for V.P. Singh. And when Rajiv Gandhi's former finance minister arrived in Bhubaneswar as the head of his Jan Morcha outfit, Biju Babu outsmarted all. (V.P. Singh's Jan Morcha, the Janata Party, the Lok Dal and the Congress (S) would eventually merge to form the Janata Dal in 1988.)

V.P. Singh's visit had raised huge expectations and a noisy, excited crowd had collected at the airport to receive him. In the front row of the waiting crowd was the soft-spoken, much-respected veteran Odisha politician Banka Behari Das.

Once the state finance minister, Das had positioned himself as V.P. Singh's frontman in Odisha. He would regularly address the press and send out press statements outlining the Jan Morcha's plans in the state. Biju Babu, then in the Janata Party, was the tallest opposition leader in Odisha, but he was not V.P. Singh's point person in the state. But as V.P. Singh disembarked from the plane and reached the terminal, Biju Babu literally elbowed everyone out. Such was his personality that few could stand up to him. Never shy of hogging the limelight, he hijacked

V.P. Singh and made him sit in his jeep. Others, Banka Babu included, watched in disbelief as he drove away with India's 'man of the moment'. Biju Babu knew that he had to hitch his wagon to V.P. Singh in order to succeed at the polls. Sure enough, the Janata Dal won the 1990 state polls and Biju Babu was back after over three decades as chief minister.

But before that, Banka Babu was distraught. That night, he issued a statement that he was renouncing public life and set out on foot for a temple. He did return home later, reportedly after a lot of persuasion from his alarmed family, but his political ambitions never recovered from the jolt he received at the airport.

In power or out of power, Biju Babu, with his swashbuckling persona, always had his way. Ironically though, in his second stint as chief minister he seemed to fall back more on symbolism than substance. Perhaps age by then was catching up. He still regaled Odias with his quotable quotes. As the head of the government, he publicly declared that people should beat up corrupt officials. 'Just send me a telegram,' he proclaimed, suggesting that people were free to take the law into their own hands once they had informed him. Hundreds of telegrams poured into the chief minister's secretariat within no time and several officials had their bones broken as emboldened people set about settling personal scores.

But corruption did not diminish, and the ageing chief minister's stock declined. To save fuel costs, he declared he would cycle to work and set out in right earnest on a borrowed cycle one day, only to lose his balance and fall. The government he headed ran aground as well. When the next assembly elections were held, his government was voted out. Then began a sad chapter in the life of the state's most prominent politician. He got elected to the Lok Sabha in 1996 but could never reclaim the exalted status of the past. His Janata Dal managed to win just four Lok Sabha seats from Odisha. So when the United Front was frantically looking for a prime ministerial candidate, the choice fell on Karnataka's Deve Gowda, who had more MPs. Biju Babu was the seniormost in the group, but his claim was overlooked as he did not have the numbers. He didn't even make it as a Central minister again. Back-room machinations marked a generational shift and his one-time protégé Srikanta Jena was made a minister instead.

Biju Babu sulked and was probably crestfallen. Soon, he took ill and died in April 1997. With him died a piece of Odisha. 'Odisha is a rich state where poor people live,' he had once said. On his death, Odias felt poorer still.

Biju Babu died in Delhi. When his body was flown to Odisha, a record five lakh people turned up spontaneously for his last rites, a first for the state. Some wept hysterically while others just stood motionless. Biju Babu's body was draped with the flags of three countries – India, Russia and Indonesia – in honour of his feats. As his body was consigned to the flames at the crematorium in Swargadwar (gateway to heaven) in Puri, Odisha found itself hopelessly adrift in a sea of collective grief.

~

The father's demise led to the arrival of a tonsured and tense Naveen.

'We felt orphaned,' recalled Bijoy Mohapatra, once Biju Babu's trusted lieutenant and the powerful irrigation minister in the government he headed from 1990 to 1995, reminiscing about the days and weeks following the party patriarch's death. Alongside despair, the legions of loyalists grew increasingly anxious about their own future in a world without Biju Babu. Many felt the Janata Dal would not survive in Odisha. Their future looked bleak and despondency within the state unit of the party grew. Some then decided that desperate times needed desperate measures.

Even before Biju Patnaik's funeral pyre was lit, some of his grieving partymen had begun to plot on how best to cash in on his memory. Several of his top followers suggested that the urn containing his ashes be taken around the state so that Odias could pay their homage to him. That the real motive was political was not lost on Biju Patnaik's intensely private children. They refused and Prem Patnaik took the urn with him to Delhi.

Having lost his chief ministership in 1995, Biju Patnaik had contested Lok Sabha elections the following year from two seats – Aska in Ganjam district and Cuttack. He won both but retained Aska and gave up the Cuttack seat. On his death, a by-election was to be held in Aska and his partymen looked for a suitable candidate to fill his shoes.

Elections in 1996 had been particularly vicious for Biju Babu's Janata Dal. As mentioned earlier, the party won just four seats in Odisha, including the two won by Biju Babu himself, and party leaders were less than optimistic about their poll prospects in the months leading up to the Aska by-poll. Their first choice for a candidate was V. Sugnana Kumari Deo, a political veteran and a scion of the erstwhile Khallikote royal family. But still smarting from her loss against Prime Minister P.V. Narasimha Rao from Berhampur the previous year, she refused. Feelers were then sent to another senior leader, Ram Krushna Patnaik. He, too, turned down the offer, fearing an inevitable electoral defeat.

As the deadline for the nomination drew close, followers of Biju Patnaik held frantic parleys at Srikanta Jena's official residence in Delhi on Pandara Road. 'The more talks were held, the more we realized the urgency for resurrecting the dead Biju,' admitted a top leader who participated in those discussions. The turnout at Biju Babu's funeral was a sign of a huge sympathy wave for the late leader. It only remained to be tapped to the party's electoral advantage.

Having started out as an underling of Biju Patnaik, Jena had made it big in New Delhi. He was a powerful minister in the United Front government and harboured greater political ambitions. The grapevine has it that he undermined Biju Patnaik in his final years, hoping to wrest for himself the reins of the state unit of the party. But not many within the party in Odisha were enamoured of Jena or his crowd-pulling abilities. Instead, they were looking to find someone who could rightfully lay a claim to Biju Babu's legacy.

Even Jena had a fair inkling of his public standing in Odisha. Piqued by stories that he had plotted to keep the state Janata Dal patriarch out of the Central cabinet in his final days, some angry mourners threw slippers and the choicest abuses at Jena during Biju Babu's funeral. Faced with an existential crisis, even Jena agreed that a Patnaik scion was best suited to lead the party in the state. The stage was thus set for a Patnaik family succession.

Senior leaders from Odisha camped at Jena's Pandara Road house and feelers were sent to Biju Patnaik's children. Weeks passed before the first responses came from the family and they were not encouraging. Prem said he wasn't interested. Some insiders feel he refused as it would make him politically vulnerable given his business background. Business dealings often fall in grey areas, and though not illegal can be politically awkward. Many viewed Gita as the natural choice as she was temperamentally the closest to Biju Babu. But married to publisher Sonny Mehta, she had settled in the United States decades ago. She too said no.

Now the only option left was Naveen, the quietest and the most reticent of the three children. With each passing day the party leaders lost hope until finally they heard back from the family: Naveen had agreed to join politics and contest the by-election for his father's seat. An industrialist who knew the family well insists that Naveen wasn't pressured by his siblings to join politics. 'It was the other way around,' he claims. One night, Naveen walked up to Prem and made his intentions clear. 'Now that you and Rani [Gita's pet name] have refused, can I go to contest from Aska?' Naveen is supposed to have asked his startled brother.

Even regular visitors to Biju Babu's Delhi home seemed to know little about Naveen. He was rarely seen around the house and he never mingled with his father's political friends. As mentioned earlier, Naveen was busy party-hopping and indulging in the finer things of life. He had by then authored three coffee-table books: *A Second Paradise* (1985), on Indian courtly life from 1590 to 1947; *Desert Kingdom* (1990), on the Rajputs of Bikaner; and *The Garden of Life* (1993), a compendium on medicinal plants and species. These were published by Doubleday in the US and two of them were edited by his good friend Jacqueline Kennedy Onassis. On Jackie's 1983 visit to India, Naveen had accompanied her to Jaipur, Jodhpur, Lucknow and Hyderabad.

The immediate past of the soft-spoken Naveen appeared incompatible with politics. Naveen instilled little confidence in the Odisha leaders and few expected him to survive the rough-and-tumble of political life. As Naveen boarded a plane and headed to Odisha to file his nomination papers for his first election from Aska, most thought he would at best be a passing phenomenon. But desperate for a member of Biju Babu's family to take over his legacy, they had no other choice.

With senior party leaders such as Ram Krushna Patnaik and V. Sugnana Kumari Deo by his side,

Naveen filed his nomination papers before the returning officer in the district headquarters of Chhatrapur, a half-hour car drive from the seaside resort of Gopalpur. Somewhat overwhelmed by the turn of events, Naveen excused himself several times for quick smokes in the anteroom as officials scrutinized his papers.

The rest was easier than anyone had imagined. Since he neither spoke nor understood any Odia, Naveen rarely gave speeches and, instead, went around the constituency waving to the people. Dilip Ray, the hotelier-cum-party-veteran at whose house Biju Patnaik spent his final days, managed his election. Debasis Nayak, a young party activist, chaperoned Naveen during his first campaign.

Naveen won hands down. But a bigger war erupted behind the scenes with different factions of the party in Odisha laying claim over him.

Jena was the most influential of the state Janata Dal leaders, by virtue of being a union minister. Biju Patnaik's declining health and fading fortunes had given Jena the opportunity to network and become a minister at the Centre. He wanted Naveen to work for the Janata Dal and shore up the party's sagging fortunes in Odisha. But other state party leaders had their own ideas. Bijoy Mohapatra, for one, reportedly held a grudge against Jena. Jena had become a union minister in 1996 by getting Mohapatra and MLAs loyal to him to lobby for him. Allegedly the deal was that once Jena became a minister, he would help Mohapatra become the Odisha president of the Janata Dal by overthrowing the incumbent Ashok Das. But Jena reneged on his promise. So now Mohapatra took the initiative to float the idea of a new party, robbing Jena of the party itself. Several other leaders were also feeling stifled in the Janata Dal which Jena controlled along with Ashok Das. They all felt the time was ripe to break away and float a regional party under Naveen.

Historically, Odisha had always had an appetite for a regional outfit. Having fought long and hard for a separate state uniting Odia-speaking tracts – Odisha, when it came into being in 1936, was the first Indian province to be created on linguistic lines – Odias suspected their collective interests were often given short shrift at the national level. Even the right to transact official business in their mother tongue was hard earned, as Bengalis, who held sway over the region in the late nineteenth and early twentieth centuries, did their best to promote their language over Odia.

Up against influential neighbours, Odias had a natural longing for a powerful voice to fight for their aspirations. Biju Patnaik had played on this theme, repeatedly drawing attention to Delhi's apathy towards Odisha, even when he was a prominent leader of the Congress party that ruled the country. The longing had led to the birth of several regional outfits, right from the first Lok Sabha elections held post-Independence in 1952, when the erstwhile rajas and large landlords of the twenty-six princely states known in Odisha as Gadjats floated their own Ganatantra Parishad party. In the 1960s, regional stalwart and former chief minister Harekrushna Mahtab left the Congress to float his Jana Congress and shared power with the Swatantra Party to form the government in the state for some time. Biju Patnaik himself walked out of the Congress and started the Utkal Congress in 1970.

These regional outfits met with mixed degrees of political success. However fleeting, the Ganatantra Parishad had stints in power, as did the Jana Congress and Utkal Congress, even if it was only as a coalition partner. But Nandini Satpathy's Jagrat Odisha, which she floated after parting with the Congress and flirting with Babu Jagjivan Ram's Congress for Democracy for some time, was a non-starter. She remained her outfit's lone representative in the assembly, never failing to win a seat from her home district of Dhenkanal. Satpathy rejoined the Congress in 1989 and retired from active politics about a decade later.

The Congress had always been a dominant force in Odisha by virtue of being the oldest party. It had a long and illustrious history and some of Odisha's best-known icons such as Gopabandhu Das had been associated with it. But its dominance was never total. Regional parties always played a role and most previous Congress governments either had a thin majority or had to tie up with other parties to rule. Thus leaders such as Bijoy Mohapatra believed there was room for another regional experiment. Aside from being directionless in Odisha post Biju Babu's death, the Janata Dal was also in a shambles at the national level. In Delhi, Deve Gowda had come and gone as the prime minister of the government headed by the party. I.K. Gujral had stepped in as Gowda's successor in the United Front government, but there were enough indications that this arrangement, propped up by the Congress from outside, would not last for long.

Even Biju Babu had sensed the uncertainty during the last months of his life when he was the MP from Aska. He went to Delhi and lived in Dilip Ray's ministerial house, where a steady stream of political friends and acquaintances called on him. The guest list included Atal Bihari Vajpayee and the BJP president L.K. Advani. Over tea and snacks, they would discuss the political situation in Odisha and the BJP veterans forcefully argued that the Janata Dal had no future in the state. Following Advani's countrywide rath yatra to build the Ram Mandir in Ayodhya, the BJP was an ascendant political force and both Vajpayee and Advani advocated that Biju Patnaik join hands with them.

Biju Babu's closest aides were aware of the discussions, but the leader himself was undecided till he breathed his last. A seasoned politician, Biju Babu kept himself abreast of all political developments and the opportunities they offered. But once he passed away, the discussions got a fresh lease of life. The political future of the Janata Dal seemed bleak and a section of the Odisha unit revived the talk of merging with the BJP. The strongest proponents for merging with the saffron party were Dilip Ray, A.U. Singh Deo and Prasanna Acharya. If they had had their way, the Janata Dal Odisha unit would have joined the BJP and Naveen would possibly have ended up as the Odisha president of the BJP.

But the pro-BJP group within the Janata Dal in Odisha couldn't muster the numbers. The Congress was in power in Odisha and the Janata Dal had only 46 MLAs in a house of 147. The majority of the Janata Dal MLAs were not keen on joining the BJP. And when a drunken legislator revealed to rival leaders that he had signed a resolution that was being surreptitiously circulated to gather support for a merger with the BJP, the group led by Bijoy Mohapatra was galvanized. Soon after Biju Babu's death, Mohapatra had visited Andhra Pradesh and met the chief minister, N. Chandrababu Naidu, to study the success of his Telugu Desam Party. He felt an increasingly powerful Jena would try to undermine him within the Janata Dal after dishonouring his promise of support for state presidentship.

Mohapatra wasted no time and accelerated the efforts to float a regional party. The Odisha leaders had been in touch with the influential BJP leader Pramod Mahajan, who saw an opening for his party in Odisha, which so far had shown no interest in the BJP. Mahajan promised to bankroll the new outfit to an extent. Naveen, a newcomer into politics and no more than an MP at that time, was told about the move and he too readily came on board. The other senior party leaders planned to use him more as a mascot – a face to harness the people's goodwill for Biju Babu. An announcement was made some months later that a new regional party was being formed under the leadership of Naveen.

In between, Bijoy Mohapatra and his group spent long hours deciding on an appropriate name for the new party. Someone suggested it could be christened Janata Dal (B) – the 'B' standing for Biju. But the idea was dropped as some leaders felt the 'B' could be misconstrued as an abbreviation for Bijoy. Some others suggested the name could be Biju Dal or even Odisha Janata Dal. A prolonged bout of brainstorming followed and a consensus emerged that the most effective name would be Biju Janata Dal (BJD).

Deciding on a party symbol also proved no less challenging. Kalpataru Das, a long-time Biju aide, suggested a lock and key as the symbol. Some others felt the plough, which once was the symbol of the Utkal Congress that Biju Patnaik had floated decades ago, could serve the purpose. But then the idea of the conch hit the group. Everyone agreed that it could be a very powerful symbol in the land of Lord Jagannath, whose four symbols included the conch. The other symbols of the presiding deity were the mace, the lotus and the wheel.

Incidentally, the symbol of the Janata Dal, the party they were breaking away from, was the wheel. But with one of the lord's symbols making way for another, the founding members of the new party were confident that its passage would be smooth in a highly religious state. And as the future unfolded, their confidence was not misplaced.

The BJD was launched in December 1997 with Naveen at its helm. He had won the Aska parliamentary by-poll in May that year and had only been in politics for six-odd months. A massive rally was held in Bhubaneswar to launch the outfit. Among those who attended the show of strength were BJP leaders Saheb Singh Verma and Shatrughan Sinha. Most Janata Dal legislators in Odisha also showed up and Jena found himself left behind, with only a handful of MLAs and an emasculated party. A new party was born with the conch as its election symbol. It was destined to blow away the Congress in a short while.

2

The First Steps

Having been elected a member of Parliament, Naveen arrived in Aska, wide-eyed.

Though just an hour's drive from the commercial town of Berhampur, known for its unkempt and crowded roads, Aska was primarily rural, where most people were poor and open defecation was rampant. It fell in the district of Ganjam, notorious for what was locally known as the 'Ganjam salute', wherein hundreds of men and women lining the roads to defecate at night would stand up, to preserve their modesty, the moment the headlights of speeding vehicles fell on them and sit down again when they passed, in seemingly unending waves. Aska was close to the tranquil sea resort of Gopalpur, but it epitomized the underdevelopment and poverty that have historically plagued Odisha.

Naveen, too, was aghast and possibly held his nose at times as he negotiated Aska's serpentine roads, lined with filth and human excreta. But he was also impressed with what Aska had to offer in spite of its collective misery. For one, the region was famous for the hordes of blackbucks that roamed freely by the side of the roads and in the courtyards of houses. Naveen was smitten by their beauty but also horrified to learn that the animals were routinely killed by speeding vehicles and sometimes poached. So one of the first things he did as MP was to paint a picture of the gentle creature himself. He got some thousand prints of the painting framed with the message 'Save the Blackbucks' scrolled across. He gave these prints to schools for distribution among the students as a gift from the newly elected MP.

Though his colleagues in the party saw little political mettle in him and viewed him more as a mascot and a means to harness votes from Biju Babu's sympathizers, Naveen took to his new role in earnest. He soaked in the sights and sounds that revealed themselves during his visits to his constituency. When he first visited Aska to file his nomination papers, his sister Gita had come along to boost his morale. In most of his subsequent visits, Ram Krushna Patnaik and V. Sugnana Kumari Deo, two local political stalwarts, gave him company and showed him around.

Naveen constantly swung between delight and dismay at what he saw. On a trip to a government hospital, he was astounded to see stray dogs sauntering in and out of the wards. 'Dogs in the hospital? Unbelievable,' he repeatedly told local senior officials in the following days as images of the ill-maintained and ill-equipped hospital continued to haunt him.

What he could change was the condition of the dying Tampara Lake in Chhatrapur. The once pristine lake, 5.8 kilometres long and 670 metres wide, was being choked with the filth and garbage that the drains and nullahs flowing into it brought in. Naveen got the lake cleaned and revived, arranging money from the local area development fund at his disposal as an MP in what was possibly his second intervention as an elected representative.

Naveen was enraptured by the beauty of the Bhairavi temple at Mantridi and the Surya mandir, perched on the top of a hill near Berhampur. The hill was almost barren and he initiated a special plantation drive to turn its slopes green.

Other leaders of the party in Odisha were happy to see Naveen doing things that came naturally to him. A founder member of the Indian National Trust for Art and Cultural Heritage (INTACH), he seemed more interested in 'softer' issues and valued tradition, trees and history. The new MP, they overwhelmingly felt, was a political novice and posed no long-term threat to them.

No alarm bells rang for the state leaders who nursed bigger ambitions for themselves when Naveen became a Central minister after the United Front government fell and a BJP government led by Atal Bihari Vajpayee took over. The BJD had performed creditably in the 1998 general elections as an ally of the BJP. Ministerial berths were due to the party in the Central cabinet and Naveen, as the party chief, was seen as the natural claimant. Many thought he would be given a portfolio of little consequence. Vajpayee, in his first meeting with Naveen in Parliament, reportedly told him that he was a natural fit as the union culture minister.

Naveen, however, got a more important portfolio and became the union minister for steel and mines. His BJD colleagues in Odisha made light of it, believing it was done to honour the memory of Biju Patnaik, who had held the portfolio during the Janata Party rule between 1977 and 1980.

In being dismissive of Naveen, his colleagues showed incredible naivety. They misread him badly, taken in completely by his outward gentle behaviour. He was prim and proper and always respectful of others. When meeting senior leaders, he always stood up and responded with warmth. He pestered them with questions about Odisha, its people and politics in general and seemed all at sea in his new vocation.

On the few occasions that he put his foot down, the overconfident party leaders, who believed they were using him and not the other way around, failed to read the signs of what was to come.

One such instance was when the newly formed BJD was being registered with the Election Commission. As the constitution of the party was being drawn up by a group led by senior leader Trilochan Kanungo, Naveen insisted he be made founder president of the party, a position for life. The framing of the constitution was held up for weeks as Naveen refused to take no for an answer. He finally acquiesced and gave up only after being told that such a provision for a permanent president could not be allowed under the Election Commission's rules for a democratic party.

But the party's registration was held up for some more time due to another of Naveen's demands. The BJD's newly drafted constitution entrusted its political affairs committee (PAC) with the sole power of choosing candidates for elections. But Naveen sent word that he, as party president, should have the final say, insisting that he should have the power of cancelling the nomination of a candidate chosen by the PAC. The demand he made was odd, but not one party leader made much of it. The rules were amended and Naveen, finally, had his way and the registration could proceed.

To get things done the way he wanted, Naveen never raised his voice or threw a tantrum. He spoke gently, gave the impression that he didn't know too much and lulled his party colleagues into comfort. 'He acted more like a child coming to terms with a new toy that he had just acquired,' said a leader, who has observed him closely from his nascent political days. In hindsight, though, it seems Naveen was playing a longer-term game. He was crafty and calculating; he knew what he wanted and how to get it. He took small but measured steps.

With Odia names being Greek and Latin to him, there were moments of embarrassment, too. During a visit to Chandikhol, the town along the national highway halfway between Bhubaneswar and Balasore, he mistakenly referred to it as 'Chadikhol' (meaning 'open your underpants') in the middle of a public address. Another time, he was in Balasore, where he attempted to invoke the name of the state's most famous litterateur, Fakir Mohan Senapati. The long-dead Senapati hailed from Balasore and is still revered for his seminal works such as *Chha Mana Atha Guntha* and *Rebati*. But Naveen got it wrong, referring to the writer as Fakir Mohan Satpathy. It was equivalent to a Bengali politician getting Tagore's name wrong. But these harmless, and hilarious, gaffes showed Naveen as unsure, simple and still uncooked, perhaps only a ploy to further lull his potential rivals into a false sense of security.

~

When in early 1998 India was going to the polls, Naveen had been in politics for less than a year. But he had a mind of his own – indeed, he was a bit of a maverick – and he did a vanishing trick during the polls.

Politicians are at their friendly best during election times. They are open, warm and charming to journalists to get the most favourable media coverage. But Naveen was not a normal politician and did not conform to the practices of other dyed-in-the-wool politicians.

Naveen was seeking re-election to Parliament from Aska, which he had won the year before. Deployed to cover Naveen's campaign, my photographer and I landed in Aska, but the BJD candidate was nowhere to be seen. Frantic calls to his personal assistant went unanswered. We had no means of getting in touch with the candidate directly. Naveen was new to the state and I was new to him.

As the hours passed and night set in, Naveen remained elusive. We suspected that he was out campaigning somewhere, but no one seemed to know exactly where. I was beginning to panic – I had a story to file – when his rather cold and curt personal assistant finally answered the call. 'Come tomorrow at 9 a.m. in front of Mermaid hotel on Gopalpur beach. Naveen Babu will start from there,' he said, and hung up abruptly.

So at nine the next morning, the *India Today* photographer and I parked ourselves in front of the budget hotel on the beach at Gopalpur, a thirty-minute drive from Berhampur. But neither Naveen nor any of his colleagues were in sight. The wait grew longer and longer, and our desperation deeper.

Naveen's assistant was once again unreachable on the phone and the two of us had no option but to keep waiting where we were until a roadside hawker, who had been watching us for three hours, came to our rescue. Leaving his cold drinks stall, he came to enquire what we were doing. When we told him we were newspaperwallahs waiting to catch up with Naveen, he laughed at our ignorance. 'You don't know where Naveen is? Go to Oberoi Gopalpur,' he said.

So off we went to the hotel, now rechristened Mayfair Palm Beach Resort by its new owners, and marched through its gates, portico and lobby. We found our prized catch by the poolside, stretching his legs and puffing a cigarette, seemingly with no worries in the world. We were excited at having finally spotted him. He wasn't, and his face said it. 'How did you find out?' he asked, his eyebrows arched in disapproval.

Quickly regaining his composure, he promised to set out on the day's electioneering immediately and let us follow him. His initial reservations disappeared and he turned into a perfect host, stopping by the roadside every now and then to check whether we would like to have tea or if we were hungry. As we talked, some camaraderie built up. But he laid two strict conditions – we were barred from reporting that he was staying at the Oberoi and that he was smoking.

Though new to the game, Naveen was already conscious of his image. He knew his biggest draw at that point was his family lineage and his perceived innocence. Unlike the other politicians, he was untainted and unsullied. He wanted to stay clean. He did not want people to know that he was staying at a five-star hotel while seeking to be the leader of a state known for its back-breaking poverty. Nor did he want them to know that he loved to smoke. He wished to be perceived as a 'good boy' in all ways, even if it meant being a little deceitful.

His voters responded enthusiastically to what they saw in their virtuous candidate and Naveen again won handsomely. But this Lok Sabha, too, was short-lived and there was another general election the next year, in 1999. Again, he won and continued to be the union minister for steel and mines without any resistance from his ambitious BJD colleagues.

Bijoy Mohapatra, the prime mover behind the formation of the BJD, was least perturbed to see Naveen growing in stature as a politician. A long-time aide of Biju Patnaik, he had been his irrigation minister and number two in the government between 1990 and 1995. He was short and slender, but, colleagues insisted, he had tall ambitions for himself. He was a consummate politician, known for his astuteness. But he was not a people's man or a mass leader, and his influence was confined mostly to his home district of Kendrapara and the adjoining districts in coastal Odisha. His strength lay in back-room politics. He was an organization man. Most BJD MLAs were hand-picked by him and owed their loyalty to him.

Since he had the support of the majority of the legislators and was the most experienced of politicians in the fledgling BJD, Mohapatra was made the chairman of its powerful political affairs committee. Those close to Mohapatra thought he was destined to be the next Odisha chief minister. The ruling Congress was hugely unpopular and Naveen was inexperienced, besides being away in Delhi as a union minister. The chief minister's crown, they felt, was for Mohapatra to take.

With the assembly elections of 2000 drawing closer, Mohapatra was busy strategizing and selecting candidates for the impending polls. Not that the party needed much strategizing, given the unpopularity of the ruling Congress. It was said that even a bamboo pole nominated by the BJD would win the elections resoundingly against a Congress candidate. As the election date neared, Mohapatra had a spring in his step. He filed his nomination papers early for the election from his home constituency of Patkura in Kendrapara district. Other party nominees had been chosen and had also filed their papers. The stage was set for a BJD sweep of the state when the all-powerful PAC met at the New Marrion hotel in Bhubaneswar for a final stocktaking. It was the last day for filing of nominations and the deadline was only hours away when Mohapatra and other PAC members trooped into the hotel.

It was a clear, crisp day when the PAC session began. Though a union minister, Naveen was contesting the assembly election from Hinjili, in his Aska parliamentary constituency, but all of Mohapatra's men felt their leader was on course for bigger things. Even if Naveen was to become the chief minister, they knew the coveted chair would come to Mohapatra sooner or later. Mohapatra had chosen most of the candidates and they were all his men. And who hadn't heard of what N. Chandrababu Naidu had done to his father-in-law, N.T. Rama Rao (NTR), in Andhra Pradesh? NTR, the matinee idol, had won a resounding victory for his Telugu Desam Party and become chief minister for the third time, only to be dethroned by his son-in-law, who walked away with most of the legislators, the party and the chief ministership.

The PAC meeting, with all members except Naveen in attendance, continued well after lunch. At around 2 p.m., Mohapatra's mobile rang. At the other end was a frantic supporter from his home constituency in Patkura. The caller's voice was charged with emotion. What he said left Mohapatra dumbfounded. While he was chairing the PAC meeting in Bhubaneswar, Naveen, as president of the party, had cancelled Mohapatra's nomination as the candidate from Patkura and chosen another as the party candidate. With just hours left for the deadline, the new candidate, Atanu Sabyasachi, had filed his papers a little while earlier. Mohapatra was devastated. His mobile buzzed again and again with more supporters from Patkura calling to give him the news. The PAC meeting ended abruptly. All the party's top leaders were present and they expressed shock at what Naveen had done. They sought to console Mohapatra, but struggled to find the right words. Undoubtedly,

Mohapatra would one day have challenged Naveen's supremacy by exercising his clout in the party and Naveen would possibly have been bested. But Naveen had pre-empted him and, with one blow, left them all speechless.

Politics anywhere is treacherous. Friends turn foe routinely and no one really knows who is a well-wisher and who an enemy and for how long. Odisha politics was no different – it had seen its share of skulduggery and back-stabbing. But this was a new low. Naveen's supporters said it was a masterstroke. His opponents said it was Machiavellian.

Though outwardly a soft and gentle person, who constantly talked of propriety, Naveen had masterminded and executed a plot that left Mohapatra high and dry. Patkura, from where Mohapatra would have to file a new nomination to contest, was a two-hour drive from Bhubaneswar and it was already past two, with just about an hour left for the deadline to pass. There was no way he could make it there and file fresh nomination papers as an independent candidate.

The plan to deny Mohapatra a chance to contest the election had apparently been set in motion the previous night. Atanu Sabyasachi was an ordinary journalist for an Odia daily, with a political background. His father was once a legislator from Patkura long before the constituency became

Mohapatra's citadel. Taken into confidence and briefed about the plan, Sabyasachi reached Patkura with two sets of papers, one cancelling Mohapatra's nomination and the other his own nomination papers bearing Naveen's signature. He waited patiently and silently. As the deadline approached, he went in and filed the papers.

Naveen, his colleagues realized, wasn't as soft and gentle as he projected himself to be. Naveen the politician had shown the ability to outsmart the smartest of them. It was only then that they realized why Naveen had insisted, during the registration of the BJD, that the ultimate power of nominating and cancelling party candidates be vested with him and not the PAC. He had long ago worked out its utility in the future. That he was capable of plotting so much in advance struck fear among the most seasoned of politicians. What else did Naveen have up his sleeve, they must have wondered.

It was an operation steeped in stealth. Even after the event not too many people talked about it openly and Naveen escaped public censure. People continued to see him as principled and decent, unlike other politicians. There was some degree of sympathy for Mohapatra in the immediate wake and some probably disapproved of the manner in which he had been denied the chance of being in the electoral fray, but no one did anything about it. Most other PAC members were themselves contesting the elections and rebelling against the party must have been the last thing on their mind. Then, with Naveen winning a resounding mandate, it was impossible for anyone to stand up to him later.

Mohapatra himself was left with no choice but to throw his weight behind an independent candidate, Trilochan Behera, already in the fray in Patkura. Behera was a non-serious candidate and would likely have forfeited his deposit had Mohapatra been in the contest. But once Mohapatra backed him, his non-existent campaign gained a new lease of life. Though the rest of Odisha was generally indifferent to the dirty trick that had been played on Mohapatra, residents of Patkura were less forgiving. They lined the streets for miles together as Mohapatra campaigned on behalf of Behera.

Sabyasachi lost and Behera won the election from Patkura. But Mohapatra's joy was short-lived. He had hoped the independent, indebted to him for his victory, would voluntarily vacate the seat, allowing him to contest the by-election and regain what he felt was his rightful place in the assembly. But that was not to be, with Naveen outmanoeuvring him once more. Firmly ensconced in the chief minister's chair, Naveen won over the independent. For the rest of the assembly's term, the independent legislator enjoyed the good life, with the state administration bending over backwards to keep him happy, and Mohapatra never got a chance to contest a by-election from Patkura.

Four years later, Odisha went in for early assembly elections, a year ahead of schedule, and the independent MLA went into oblivion. But by then he had served his purpose and Mohapatra had been banished into political wilderness. Mohapatra contested from Patkura, but sympathy for him had long dried up. The state administration had worked hard to cultivate the constituency and this time Sabyasachi won.

Mohapatra continues to be out in the cold. In October 2000, he formed a regional outfit, the Odisha Gana Parishad, which he later merged with Sharad Pawar's Nationalist Congress Party (NCP) with an eye on the 2009 elections. But then, Naveen dealt him another debilitating blow. If in 2000 Naveen had robbed him of his party ticket, in 2009 Naveen walked away with his party itself.

As the Odisha president of the NCP, Mohapatra was hoping to stitch together an electoral alliance with all anti-Naveen forces in the state. Every other evening, he would hold press conferences and spew venom at the government that Naveen headed. Albeit the loudest anti-Naveen voice in the state, where the bigger opposition parties had largely abdicated their role, Mohapatra was little more than a one-man army. And with days to go for the elections, the NCP's central leadership dropped a bombshell, announcing that they would back Naveen in the polls. The Odisha chief minister had obviously worked his charm and Mohapatra was, once again, left stranded. He remained the state party president, but the party no more toed his line. Sitting alongside several other top state NCP leaders including Odia cine star Prashanta Nanda, Mohapatra let off another anti-Naveen rant. 'Odisha NCP will not abide by the central NCP. We will fight against Naveen,' he announced.

But Naveen again got the better of him. Less than twenty-four hours later several of the NCP leaders who had shared the stage with Mohapatra at the anti-Naveen event held another press conference. No one knows for sure what brought about their sudden change of heart, but this time the NCP leaders, Nanda included, pledged support for Naveen. Some of them were promptly rewarded for their somersault and given BJD tickets. Nanda later became an official spokesperson of the party and a BJD Rajya Sabha MP. Mohapatra is still licking his wounds, having lost successive elections to the assembly. Without a party and outwitted time and again, he joined the BJP, but failed to make a mark. Old-timers in the BJP remained suspicious of him and kept him at bay. Relations with other leaders soured and Mohapatra finally had to leave that party, too. His political marginalization has been near total. He tried every trick in the book to re-enter the assembly, but Naveen thwarted him each time with the skill of a professional assassin. This ruthless killer instinct, which would be deployed several times in the future, too, was probably why Naveen lasted very long as the chief minister.

~

With Bijoy Mohapatra, the biggest potential rival, taken care of, the rest was easy for Naveen Patnaik.

Being elected chief minister for the first time in 2000 was easy for Naveen since the Congress had been in power in Odisha for the previous five years and its rule, rather misrule, had made it hugely unpopular. The Congress's fall from grace in the state was both dramatic and drastic. For much of contemporary history, the party had been a dominant political force and had footprints all across the state. Its legacy was to be found everywhere and its exploits were legendary. Gopabandhu Das, Odisha's first Congress president, is deeply revered even today. So is Nabakrushna

Choudhury, the state's second Congress chief minister. Local folklore has it that the day he ceased to be the chief minister in 1956, he took a rickshaw home from his official residence.

But the party's immediate past was less illustrious. Since the 1980s, the Congress had come to be dominated by J.B. Patnaik. A renowned scholar whose erudition no one challenged, J.B. Patnaik had been the editor of a local daily, *Prajatantra*. Then he entered electoral politics and got into the good books of Indira Gandhi, who made him a junior union minister. In 1980, he became Odisha's chief minister for the first time and continued to be in power until late 1989. But his tenure was marked by broken promises and a steady stream of controversies. He pledged '1000 industries in 1000 days', but there was little evidence of any new investments on the ground. He constantly made news for all the wrong reasons. He was suspected of trying to hush up the story when Chabirani, the wife of a journalist, was gang-raped and killed. His promises to pull Odisha out of poverty came to nought and the state slipped deeper into hunger and destitution. Midway into his term, a story broke that Panas Punji, a tribal woman in the state's drought-ravaged Kalahandi district, had sold her young niece Banita for as little as ₹60 to a blind man. The story shook the nation's conscience and Kalahandi came to be seen as India's equivalent of the then famine-stricken Ethiopia.

As the national press pilloried Patnaik, his standing plummeted. Then came the *Illustrated Weekly of India*'s exposé of his supposed sexual escapades. The story never stood up to scrutiny, but Patnaik's stock nosedived anyway. He would have lost the elections in 1985, but Prime Minister Indira Gandhi's assassination triggered a nationwide sympathy wave and Patnaik was its beneficiary in Odisha. He got re-elected as chief minister and the state continued its downward slide. Lawlessness ruled and lumpenization became rampant as a group of J.B. Patnaik's family members and their associates seized the reins of power. Odias resented his rule, but they could do little about it. J.B. Patnaik had, by then, totally monopolized the party machinery and had the high command under his thumb. He was forced to step down in 1989 as a worried Congress leadership attempted to retrieve lost ground before the 1990 assembly elections. The Congress lost the elections and Biju Patnaik won, but J.B. Patnaik did not fade away.

Biju Patnaik too did not succeed in changing the fortunes of the state between 1990 and 1995. But mindful of J.B. Patnaik's unpopularity, a chastised Congress played its cards well in the 1995 elections. It refrained from naming a chief ministerial candidate.

Instead, it chose union minister Giridhar Gamang, a tribal leader from the southern district of Koraput, as the campaign committee chairman. Gamang led from the front and it created the impression that he would be the chief minister if the Congress won. It did win, but Gamang didn't get to occupy the prized chair. As the results were being declared and Congress candidates kept winning, J.B. Patnaik sent out both cars and men to ferry the victorious MLAs to a Bhubaneswar safe house. By the time the high command sent its emissary to choose the chief minister, J.B. Patnaik had the majority of the legislators under his control and was in a position to hijack the victory for himself. 'Though never popular, he was the best manager the Congress ever had,' a party old-timer said. J.B. Patnaik had no problems being elected the leader of the Congress legislative party. No one opposed him and J.B. Patnaik's men celebrated. A sizeable section of Odias were left stunned.

Many found it difficult to digest that J.B. Patnaik was back at the helm, although through the back door. Most felt uneasy about the future. Many suffered from a sense of guilt, having voted against Biju Patnaik's Janata Dal. Odias had reservations about Biju Babu's rule between 1990 and 1995, but they still had respect and love for him. A waiter at the ITDC Ashok Hotel in Bhubaneswar seemed to echo popular sentiment when he said remorsefully, 'We wanted to punish him, but not banish him. If only we had known that J.B. Patnaik would be the chief minister, we would have voted otherwise.'

Few had any expectations from the new Congress government to begin with and J.B. Patnaik's latest tenure went along expected lines, with the chief minister focusing on self-preservation. Governance took a back seat and fresh rounds of scandals and controversies erupted every now and then. Things got particularly ugly when a young, articulate woman, Anjana Mishra, levelled charges of sexual assault against Indrajit Ray, the state's advocate general and a J.B. Patnaik confidant. Mishra was embroiled in a marital dispute with her husband, who was an officer in the Indian Forest Service. It was a private battle and ought to have stayed so. But rather mysteriously, her case file ended up with Ray and he called her over for discussions. Mishra came out of the meeting levelling serious charges against the state's highest legal officer. J.B. Patnaik was in no way involved, but he got drawn into the controversy as he refused to sack Ray for months. Temperatures rose, with political parties joining in and accusing the government of shielding Ray. Though J.B. Patnaik finally relented and ordered Ray to step down, matters got infinitely worse when

Mishra later alleged that she was waylaid on her way to Cuttack one night and gang-raped. This time, she accused J.B. Patnaik of orchestrating the assault to silence her.

All hell broke loose and what essentially started out as a private dispute acquired political dimensions. The opposition parties and ordinary people took to the streets, venting their anger by targeting Congress and government offices. As J.B. Patnaik's name was dragged through the mud, he kept insisting on his innocence. Though J.B. Patnaik seemed to have been shielding Ray, it must be said that he stood to gain nothing from the assault on Mishra. But the incident only provided further ammunition to the opposition and to his detractors within the party. Few paid any heed to him or to what he said in his defence. Whatever was left of the Congress popularity crashed further.

Controversies of a sexual nature dogged J.B. Patnaik. And the rumours got reinforced in the public mind when none other than a former director general of police, Amiya Bhushan Tripathy, took the stand before a judge in the high court as a witness in a public interest litigation over the case involving Mishra, and levelled a more damaging allegation against the chief minister. Asked to depose by the court, Tripathy dropped a bombshell. He claimed in his testimony that the chief minister shared with the former advocate general a 'passion for women'.

In between, there was another sexual controversy involving the wife of a Congress partyman who died suspiciously in a road accident. As always, J.B. Patnaik found himself in the thick of it. Rumour-mongers had a field day and insinuations of complicity at the highest level did the rounds.

J.B. Patnaik's reputation was ruined beyond repair. And then in early 1999 the Australian missionary Graham Staines and his two young children were burnt alive while they slept in their car out in the open in Manoharpur near Thakurmunda in the predominantly tribal Mayurbhanj district. The gruesome murders that made international news were the handiwork of a freelance Hindu zealot called Dara Singh, but many held J.B. Patnaik responsible. Despite his strong links with central leaders, the Congress high command could not take it any more. State elections were just a year away and the party tried to put its house in order. Patnaik finally made way for Gamang as the chief minister.

But the choice turned out to be no less disastrous. Gamang was an affable tribal leader from Koraput and had been winning elections to the Lok Sabha without a break from the 1970s. He was mostly away in Delhi as an MP. As the telecom minister under

Rajiv Gandhi, the sheen of the telecom revolution that was witnessed across the country had rubbed off on him, though those in the know said that the credit should go to Rajiv Gandhi's favourite technocrat, Sam Pitroda, who incidentally was born in Balangir district of Odisha.

Gamang had the reputation of being a simple, modest man. Even after becoming the chief minister, he would often visit homes of acquaintances to attend family functions and sit on the floor with other guests to have meals. However, he fell short of being an able administrator and a quick decision maker. Though a long-time MP, he had spent most of his time either in Koraput or in Delhi, only passing through Bhubaneswar in transit, and hence he was unfamiliar with the power centres of the capital and the way they worked. The majority of the sitting Congress MLAs were J.B. Patnaik men and the loyalty of the bureaucrats also lay with the outgoing chief minister. Gamang sought to bring in his people, but the establishment was tough to change. He shuffled and reshuffled officials incessantly. But over time, his indecisiveness took its toll and the administration faltered. Dara Singh, still on the run, wreaked more havoc. A Christian priest and a Muslim trader were among those Dara Singh went on to murder, and large tracts of Odisha seemed to be swept by lawlessness.

Gamang wasn't a hated figure, but he didn't endear himself to the people either. The last remnants of his reputation were swept away when a killer cyclone crept up the Bay of Bengal and hit the state on the night of 29 October 1999. The winds that the cyclone packed in the eye of the storm travelled at 250 kilometres an hour. The supercyclone battered the state, scooping up the sea in some places. In Ersama in Jagatsinghpur district in coastal Odisha, waves more than 20 feet high rushed some 22 kilometres inside, sweeping away all that came in the way. Houses were flattened, trees uprooted and electric polls smashed. Some 10,000 people died in the state and the cost, in terms of loss of property and infrastructure, came to thousands of crores.

As the storm abated, Odisha found itself drowning in misery. Hundreds of thousands were hungry, with aid and relief nowhere in sight. There wasn't even wood available to cremate the soaked and bloated bodies that floated up as the water receded. The winds had toppled electric and telephone poles and most of Odisha, Bhubaneswar included, plunged into darkness. Both landlines and mobile phones went dead. The control tower at Bhubaneswar airport had been knocked out of service and no planes could land. Train services, too, remained disrupted for days. As hunger and despair rose, panic set in. With rumours having a free run in the absence of news from the state's interiors, everyone feared the worst for their families staying in their native villages. Thousands of policemen deserted their posts and began trekking back to their home towns, even as desperate locals began targeting the few trucks stranded on the highways. Madness took over and residents looted whatever they could lay their hands on, including trucks carrying cement and condoms. An already lax administration simply abdicated and anarchy took over.

The scale of the disaster was such that dealing with it effectively would have stretched even the best-run administration in the country. The administration headed by Gamang simply stood no chance. That a monstrous storm was headed towards the state was predicted well in advance. But Gamang believed in the gods and the night before the killer cyclone hit, he chose to closet himself with three godmen from Puri. What transpired that night at the chief minister's official residence would have gone down as the most comic moment in administrative history if the fate that befell the state had not been so tragic. Officials present recall the godmen acting as soothsayers and being at their sycophantic best. They competed with one another to please the chief minister. Poring over the chief minister's horoscope, one godman said

Gamang's star constellations were such that the cyclone would pass 'high' over Odisha, sparing the territory. Another said the storm would break into two, one heading to neighbouring Andhra Pradesh and the other towards West Bengal. No damage would be done to Odisha, he predicted. If any medals were at stake that night though, the third godman would have got the gold. He insisted the storm would rebound on hitting the short-statured chief minister's chest and return to the sea without causing any destruction.

Gamang is said to have gone to sleep that night adequately comforted. When he woke up the next morning, he found himself under siege. Giant trees had fallen and blocked his gate. His staff had forgotten to stock diesel for the generator and there was no power at home. All phone lines were dead. For once, the chief minister who loved to talk non-stop was struck dumb. The severity of the disaster finally dawned on him, but it was too late. It took weeks to restore the infrastructure and organize relief. Battered and bruised, Odisha found itself afloat on a sea of despair as the waves receded to the sea.

The only ones who found a ray of hope amid the all-pervasive hopelessness were Gamang's rivals within the Congress. Still smarting under the humiliation of being stripped of his position some months ago, J.B. Patnaik once again rallied his men and directed his ire at Gamang and a sizeable section of Congress legislators now demanded that Gamang be replaced. 'Go-man-go,' they made fun of Gamang, as they lobbied with the party high command to sack him. With the ruling party's stock at its lowest and elections just months away, the central leadership relented. They let go of Gamang and chose Hemananda Biswal.

Biswal continued as the chief minister for three months, until the elections, but the Congress never had any real chance of salvaging anything. It had gained the reputation of being corrupt, incompetent and inept. So by the time Naveen Patnaik took off in the twin-engine helicopter to campaign for his BJD–BJP alliance – the anecdote with which this book began – there was a groundswell of support building for him across the disillusioned state. All that Naveen was required to do was to tell the expectant crowds that he would do everything he could to fulfil his father Biju Patnaik's unfulfilled dreams and daintily wave at them. No one pressed him to explain what his father's dreams were or what his plans were to realize them.

Fulfilling Biju Patnaik's dreams had remained a constant theme for the BJD government over successive terms. In 2016–17, when the Odisha government celebrated Biju Babu's birth centenary with gusto, BJD workers and Naveen renewed their pledge to realize the late patriarch's dreams. '*Biju babunka swapna ame sakaar kariba*' (We will convert Biju Babu's dreams into reality) declared the posters and placards put up by the party through the year-long celebrations. It did not matter that only two years ago, in 2014, a local activist, Pradip Pradhan, had asked for an answer from the government under the Right to Information (RTI) Act on what Biju Babu's dreams meant. The chief minister's office gave a matter-of-fact reply: no documents existed on Biju Babu's dreams. But such small details never really mattered. They definitely did not matter back in 2000 when Odisha saw Naveen as its only saviour and a surge of popular support swept him to power.

3

The Uninterrupted Reign

Naveen Niwas, the sprawling home that Biju Patnaik built and named after his youngest son just beyond Bhubaneswar airport, was unusually quiet, while excitement, bordering on mass hysteria, swept the rest of Odisha.

Forest Park, the fashionable neighbourhood next to Naveen Niwas, was no exception. Home to top bureaucrats, retired and serving, and other well-to-do families, the upscale part of the city shared the day's excitement. As the day progressed and the results of the 2000 elections to the Odisha assembly began streaming in, people began to step out of their homes. Roadside tea stalls did brisk business and the tin-box kiosks that sold cigarettes and paan had crowds gathering in front of each of them. Everyone discussed the results and no one had any doubt that Naveen Patnaik, leading the BJD–BJP alliance, was headed for a landslide victory.

But inside Naveen Niwas, the man at the centre of it all was calm. He was also pretty much alone. But for his personal staff of cooks and gardeners, the house, complete with marble floors, exquisitely carved statues and a wide spiral staircase, was empty. Though a union minister entitled to a retinue of staff, Naveen had, as usual, given them time off during elections. Naveen valued propriety and took every precaution in the book not to be seen doing anything remotely improper. His partymen were also away, contesting elections or keeping an eye on the counting process in their own constituencies. Naveen sat at one end of a long dining table, his favourite spot, and kept track of the results on the television over occasional cups of coffee and endless cigarettes. A smattering of a spirited crowd began to gather outside his gate, but Naveen was cool and composed. Giving him company at the dining table were two journalists. I was one of them.

Electronic voting machines (EVMs) had not yet been introduced and the manual counting of ballots took considerable time. Final results were still a long time away, but early trends relayed by local television channels made it clear that the BJD–BJP alliance was making huge gains. Though the BJP was in power in Delhi with Atal Bihari Vajpayee as the prime minister, the BJD, claiming to be the repository of goodwill for Biju Patnaik, was the senior partner in the coalition. For all the support, in terms of morale and money, that it had provided at the time of the formation of the BJD, the BJP had been allotted only 63 assembly seats from which to contest while the BJD fielded candidates from the remaining 84 seats.

The two parties complemented each other, harnessing the sympathy and support that existed for the late Biju Patnaik, while tapping into the goodwill that Prime Minister Vajpayee enjoyed. Though never a bastion of the BJP, Odisha had also come under the resurgent Hindutva spell that seemed to have captured the rest of India following the demolition of the Babri Masjid. Odisha was free of any polarization on communal lines. Muslims were concentrated in certain pockets such as Bhadrak and Cuttack, accounting for no more than 2 per cent of the population. The often pensive Vajpayee, the poet-politician, was riding the crest of popularity. His deputy, Lal Krishna Advani, was seen as a man of action in the mould of Sardar Vallabhbhai Patel.

Odisha sends 21 MPs to the Lok Sabha and in the parliamentary elections of 1998 and 1999, Odias had made their choice clear. The BJD and BJP had fought both the elections together, the BJD contesting in 12 seats and the BJP in 9. And on both occasions, the BJP–BJD combine swept the polls. In 1998, the BJD won 9 seats it contested while the BJP was victorious in 6. In 1999, they did even better, with the BJD winning 10 of the 12 seats it contested and the BJP winning all its 9 seats.

The 1998 and 1999 parliamentary polls were seen as a sort of semi-final ahead of the more coveted assembly elections, and the outcome of the 2000 vote was never really in doubt. The possibility of any sudden switch in popular mood was so remote that a despondent Congress had given up even before the first ballot was cast. On a flight back to Bhubaneswar from Delhi just three days ahead of the polls, a senior state Congress minister was frank enough to speak his mind aloud. 'We are losing,' he said. 'We will have to sit at home for the next five years.' His confession was both right and wrong. The Congress lost badly, winning just 26 seats. But the minister was way off the mark when he predicted its banishment would last only five years. The minister and his party colleagues were made to sit at home for decades.

At Naveen's home on counting day, no one had any inkling that the change taking place would be so long-lasting. Dilip Ray, a union minister and the senior BJD leader at whose house Biju Patnaik had breathed his last, paid a visit and both he and Naveen congratulated each other. Neither showed any emotion. But an hour or so later, Nalinikanta Mohanty, the working president of the BJD, dropped in for a while. By then, more results had come in and Naveen couldn't control himself. As Mohanty congratulated him for the grand showing, Naveen's eyes turned moist – just for a fleeting moment.

Soon, it was back to Naveen and just the two of us, the journalists. Lunch was spartan and consisted of some hot soup, bread and a small piece of fried fish. Meal over, Naveen went back to watching television. The crowd gathering outside was swelling by the hour and many of them now wanted to see him. Bouquets and sweets had begun to flood the home of the leader now set to take over as the state's new chief minister. But Naveen did not step out past his tastefully decorated drawing room into the portico even once. Only after dusk did he change his clothes and finally get into a rented cab to be driven for a kind of a victory lap around the television studios. His first stop was the state information centre, then called Soochana Bhavan and now Jaydev Bhavan, for a live interview with Doordarshan. Then he visited the studios of private broadcasters for more interviews. On the day he was crowned by the people, Naveen did not have a ministerial car, official staff or a siren-blaring pilot vehicle. As he zipped across the city, sitting in the front next to the driver, I occupied the back seat and had a ringside view of the change that was unfolding in the state.

The Odisha that Naveen was due to take over looked bleak. Utter poverty and chronic underdevelopment plagued the state prone to natural disasters. Corruption was widespread and scandals rife. Many people blamed the vested interests firmly entrenched in Bhubaneswar and the state's all-powerful bureaucracy. Senior officials enjoyed perks, privileges and status unmatched in the rest of the country, to the extent that even a roadside vendor in those times could tell who the home secretary or the works secretary was. A few well-connected families virtually made all the decisions and prospered, cornering government contracts and business deals. With Naveen in the driver's seat finally, people prayed for things to change.

Many saw Naveen as the 'stranger chief minister'. Few in Odisha knew who he was, what he was or what made him tick. The prospective chief minister also knew precious little about Odisha or Odias and their way of life even though he had visited the state often since becoming an MP and a union minister. But they pinned their hopes on Naveen and waited for him to deliver.

~

Naveen took over as chief minister and came to live in Bhubaneswar permanently. He had shed his jeans and T-shirt for the politicians' kurta-pyjama long ago, but now, as he began to hold a daily durbar at his home, he switched to wearing the famous lungi from Khordha, the town located not far from Bhubaneswar. As Naveen held court in the morning, sitting at the head of his dining table, only a select group of senior party leaders had access to him. He pestered them with his pet line – '*Aur batao* (Tell me more)' – as he sought to know more about the state that now has come to be his home. In the early days of his chief ministership, one regular early morning guest was Rajkishore Das, a retired Odia teacher, employed by partymen who thought it would serve the leader well if he quickly learnt the local language. But while Naveen was keen to learn more about the places and people of Odisha from those who visited him, Das was mostly ignored and sat idle, sipping coffee and reading newspapers until he finally stopped coming one day. 'Why does the teacher come when you are not interested in learning your mother tongue?' asked one of Naveen's bureaucrat aides one day. 'When was Odia my mother tongue?' Naveen is said to have retorted in lighter vein, alluding to his mother, Gyan, who was a Punjabi. But the new chief minister persisted with Das for months. It apparently was good for public perception. Naveen calculated that the people would be happy to know that he was taking Odia lessons, however sham it was. Also, he had learnt that the teacher was a part-time astrologer and he occasionally made use of him in the name of tuitions.

The new chief minister, personal staff said, had set habits. He would start the day with a glass of orange juice, a few slices of watermelon or papaya and a cup of coffee. Then he would get busy meeting those who came into his dining room, lighting up one cigarette after another. When he left for the state secretariat around 11 a.m., he would have a glass of coconut water. He would return home for a very light lunch, mostly khichdi and a bowl of curd or simply bread and soup, and head back to the office. Returning home past dusk, he would settle down for a drink of Famous Grouse whisky after 9 p.m., though Article V (B2) of the 37-page BJD party constitution stipulated that 'party members should abstain from alcoholic drinks and drugs'. Dinner was the time when Naveen would indulge himself, with his only proper meal of the day. Red hot Thai chicken curry was said to be one of his favourites.

For a one-time party animal, Naveen lived a rather lonely life in Bhubaneswar. He led the entire state, but had few for company at home. There were not too many people in Bhubaneswar the suave, chain-smoking, English-speaking chief minister could relate to and the only two people who dropped in frequently to share a drink with him at home in the initial years were the veteran politician A.U. Singh Deo and the industrialist-turned-politician Baijayant 'Jay' Panda. Both had illustrious family backgrounds, were widely connected and spoke smooth, accented English like Naveen. They met regularly during the evenings and engaged in small talk over drinks. Naveen, by then, had come to entertain himself by giving names to prominent politicians and officials. He curiously named them after animals, and one chief minister of a neighbouring state had been named 'Chipmunk'. 'What is the latest about the chipmunk?' he would ask his amused companions in zest. A portly Odisha politician had been named 'Toad', while he preferred to call a particularly tall official 'Giraffe'. Other guests who made it past the portico and into the living quarters at Naveen Niwas were never made to feel they were unwanted. Yet, from very early in his tenure, Naveen let it be known to everyone that he was for no one, despite his show of warmth and courtesy.

The new chief minister seemed delighted when visitors such as the portly Braja Bhai, the all-powerful general manager of the largest and most powerful Odia daily *Samaja*, came calling. Lacking any worthwhile formal education, Braja Bhai spoke no English and seemed a bit crass. His visiting card had a photograph of him. Having come to control *Samaja*, Braja Bhai enjoyed being in the news himself. Every time he left for Delhi, *Samaja*'s front page would scream '*Braja Bhai Gale*' (Braja Bhai has left) alongside a photograph of him being given a warm send-off at the airport or railway station by his fawning staff. '*Braja Bhai Asile*' (Braja Bhai has arrived), the paper would religiously proclaim when he returned.

Braja Bhai loved attention and Naveen showered him with plenty when he visited Naveen Niwas one day. 'Braja Bhai is here,' the chief minister informed his officials and colleagues, letting the world know he had an important guest. Perhaps Naveen was trying to flatter Braja Bhai. In those days, *Samaja*'s influence was unmatched and politicians of all parties competed with one another to keep its bosses in good humour. Many VIPs also made it a habit to visit the paper's office, along with the mandatory trip to the Jagannath temple in Puri, on important occasions such as taking oath as a minister. Since it made sense to butter up Braja Bhai, he was plied with tea, coffee and snacks at Naveen Niwas. When Braja Bhai left that day, Naveen went up to the portico to see him off. Some months later, the same Braja Bhai lost control of the paper and found himself in jail on charges of misappropriating company funds. He spent months in jail but Naveen didn't come forward to bail him out. That's Naveen for you.

Politicians of all hues did their best to impress Naveen. They often went to great lengths to project their apparent closeness to him. One particular politician would come visiting often. When he walked through the gate and the portico, watched by the gathered partymen and favour-seekers, he would be ramrod straight. But once inside the drawing room, he would begin to cower and by the time he reached the dining room he would practically be crawling. On his way out, he would gradually straighten up and walk out, full of himself. Though initially outraged by the show of sycophancy, Naveen gradually got used to it. In the early years, he would grimace when senior leaders would stoop to touch his feet. Two years later, the same Naveen made a face when a legislator from Cuttack district came but did not bend fully to bow before him. He did not like that the MLA had not paid him full obeisance.

Though partymen were still in the process of figuring out Naveen, they had begun to worship him. Soon, they would come to fear him. An abrupt downturn in the political fortunes of two senior BJD leaders, people who could perhaps some day have emerged as potential rivals to Naveen, helped spread the fear. The killer instinct that was on display when Naveen cut Bijoy Mohapatra to size came to the fore again soon after he became chief minister.

The first casualty was Dilip Ray, the union minister in whose house Biju Patnaik breathed his last and who managed Naveen's first parliamentary election. A businessman-politician, Ray was a senior leader with stature, resources and contacts. He was one of Odisha's richest politicians, with declared assets of more than ₹100 crore. Above all, many of Biju Patnaik's followers were grateful to him for having stood by their leader during his final days, when many other leaders had abandoned him. Given his financial muscle and the emotional connect he enjoyed with partymen, Ray could some day have emerged as a parallel power centre within the BJD. But in May 2000, Naveen asked Prime Minister Vajpayee to induct into his ministry two junior leaders from the BJD. Ray figured that his days were numbered – after all alliance partners are given a fixed number of ministerial offices – and resigned from the union cabinet. His political career nosedived after that. He ultimately left the BJD, helping Naveen to consolidate his position. Naveen barely had to exert himself but, master of symbolism and subtle hints, he got what he wanted.

The other prominent leader to fall by the wayside as the new chief minister stamped his authority was Nalinikanta Mohanty, BJD's working president and second only to Naveen in the party hierarchy. In July 2001 when Mohanty, Naveen's works, housing and urban development minister, was watching television at his secretariat office in the evening, preparing to go home, local television channels broke the story of a brief communiqué issued by the office of the chief minister, just one floor above in the same building. Quoting from the communiqué, the channels said the chief minister had just written to the governor to sack three of his senior ministers from the cabinet. Mohanty was one of them, the other two being Kamala Das and Prashanta Nanda. In the statement and in television interviews that he subsequently gave that night, Naveen said the three had come under a 'shadow of corruption' and he was forced to act. He refused to explain further and retreated into his official chambers.

The surgery to remove the three was planned and executed in stealth, and was primarily aimed at delivering a shock-and-awe treatment to all elected BJD ministers and legislators who could have been silently nursing ambitions to topple the novice Naveen sooner or later by organizing a rebellion. The list of three was drawn up some three days before the state governor was notified to sack them. On the day the governor was to be informed, the then state chief secretary was called into the chief minister's office and informed about what was to happen. A portly man with a fair degree of appetite, the chief secretary was made to sit in the office until the operation was over. He was not allowed to leave and forced to munch biscuits for lunch. The stunned chief secretary signed the notifications and another senior officer carried them to the equally surprised governor. The governor signed and the sackings came into effect. The chief secretary left for a much-delayed lunch only in the evening.

As with Bijoy Mohapatra who was denied the party ticket at the last moment, Mohanty, too, was shocked by the suddenness of what had struck him. After a while, he tried climbing up the stairs to the chief minister's secretariat for an explanation. But by then, security on the third floor of the building had been tightened. There were more policemen than usual and not even a fly was being let in. Mohanty left his office shaken. He never returned. A six-time MLA from Rajnagar in coastal Odisha, the constituency Biju Babu had once represented, Mohanty joined the Congress and won a re-election to the assembly. But that was that. He never occupied any important official position again and died – many say of heartbreak – a few years later.

The deed was done and another potential party rival was done away with. Corruption cases were filed against all three ministers in 2002 after a vigilance enquiry which was completed in less than a year. In

2010, Kamala Das was convicted by a special vigilance court and awarded two years' rigorous imprisonment and fined ₹4000.

The swift and sudden takedown of his virtual number two had the desired effect and no one in the party dared raise their voice against him. The people's faith in Naveen, however, rose. That he had sacked three powerful ministers reinforced his image as someone who tolerated no transgressions.

Naveen went on to burnish his anti-graft, no-nonsense reputation further when he sent home half a dozen powerful officers of the Indian Administrative Service (IAS). In a sudden move, he stripped the bureaucrats, viewed as dishonest and inefficient, of their powers. 'You are no more required,' Naveen told the IAS officers, even withdrawing their official cars. 'You've got no work, so no car is required.' Odisha had never seen anything of this kind and Naveen's stock with the public skyrocketed. The move served twin purposes – the chief minister's popularity grew and the bureaucracy, which could be recalcitrant, fell in line.

As Naveen went about consolidating his position, so did another gentleman residing in the bustling part-residential, part-commercial neighbourhood of Saheed Nagar at the other end of the city. Pyari Mohan Mohapatra was a retired bureaucrat who had once served as secretary to Biju Patnaik when he was the chief minister. Though imperious and haughty, he had the reputation of being an able administrator. He also had the trust of the senior Patnaiks. The grapevine has it that when Naveen made his way to Odisha as a politician, Gyan Patnaik advised her son to take Mohapatra's counsel since he knew no one else. So Naveen sought out Pyari Mohapatra, asking him for advice on matters of administration and to check out on politicians and bureaucrats. In the beginning, it was all hush-hush and the two rarely met in public. Insiders say they preferred to speak on the phone. Then Pyari Mohapatra took to routinely faxing his views and advice to the chief minister. On matters of transfers and postings of officials in politically crucial positions, from senior police officials to tehsildars in the blocks, select bureaucrats at the chief minister's office would visit Pyari Mohapatra for consultations. Other routine administrative matters were looked after by a few hand-picked bureaucrats, known for their honesty and efficiency. The arrangement benefited an 'inexperienced' Naveen. It allowed him time to find his feet in the 'new' state and his moorings in politics.

Pyari Mohapatra's stature grew with every passing day and soon he came to be seen as the state's 'super chief minister'. The arrangement caused heartburn among many, especially those who saw themselves as close to Naveen. A typical example was Debasis Nayak. He was in Naveen's charmed circle in his initial years in politics. As someone who ran errands for Biju Patnaik, he had come to know Naveen and did odd jobs for him too, tending to small things such as ushering in guests and getting documents photocopied. He was rewarded for his loyalty. Given an assembly ticket, he won as a BJD candidate and became a minister in Naveen's first cabinet. But his authority declined in proportion to the rise in Pyari Mohapatra's influence. Soon, Nayak turned bitter. 'Pyari Mohapatra is to Naveen what Mayawati was to Kanshi Ram and Kusum Rai was to Kalyan Singh,' he told the *India Today* magazine, referring to the controversial relationships the founder of the Bahujan Samaj Party and the former chief minister of Uttar Pradesh had with their respective party leaders. Nayak was miffed that Pyari Mohapatra had become all too powerful, just as Mayawati and Kusum Rai were during the heyday of their mentors.

An impression gained ground that Naveen was a mere facade and that the real power lay with Pyari Mohapatra. A few well-informed bureaucrats, however, saw through the clever ploy of the new chief minister. The arrangement allowed him to stay in the background, consolidate power and take credit for positive achievements, while Pyari Mohapatra took the blame for anything that went wrong and for the dirty work that politics involved. Many, in fact, blamed Mohapatra for the denial of a ticket to Bijoy Mohapatra and the dismissal of Nalinikanta Mohanty from the union cabinet. 'What, after all, does Naveen know? He is so new,' a retired engineer residing in Bhubaneswar said, echoing popular sentiment. Pyari Mohapatra, instead, was pilloried for 'settling his own personal scores'. The retired bureaucrat was known to have a huge ego and he enjoyed the sight of politicians and officials queuing up before his house for an audience. He willingly took the blame for the political machinations, though Naveen happened to be their biggest beneficiary.

The arrangement, in hindsight, suited both Naveen and Pyari Mohapatra. Naveen had all his potential rivals cut down to size one by one. Pyari Mohapatra enjoyed exercising power and took pride in the growing perception that he determined the destiny of even the seniormost party leaders. He began to believe he was consolidating his hold over the chief minister, the party and the state administration. Naveen pretended to know little or nothing. He portrayed an image of a non-interfering simpleton. But everything that was needed to be done to strengthen him got done without fail. Only much later did partymen,

Pyari Mohapatra included, realize that Naveen had been a master strategist even when he was new to politics.

Naveen's non-interfering style had many advantages. It helped shape his personal image to a great extent. It also brought about a huge change in the way the administration in Odisha was run. One day early in his tenure, the Odisha assembly was in session when MLAs, cutting across party lines, were up in arms. Mahima Mishra, a local industrialist with deep pockets and wide political connections, had been arrested by the state crime branch and the legislators took to the floor of the House to express their displeasure. 'This is an attack on Odia pride,' complained an enraged BJD MLA. Naveen was in the assembly building, but not in the House. Sitting in his chief ministerial chambers in the assembly, he heard the din inside the House and enquired what the commotion was. When an official briefed him, an unperturbed Naveen asked, 'But who is this Mahima Mishra?' refusing to intervene and indicating that the authorities were free to do their duty.

Confident that their new chief minister, unlike his predecessors, favoured no one, bureaucrats and the police went about their business unencumbered by any constraints. They arrested goons, cracked down on malpractices of contractors and attempted to play by the book. A collector of a politically sensitive district has an interesting story to tell. Towards the end of the Congress rule, a few months before Naveen took over, the district police had arrested and jailed a notorious gangster with a long criminal record and links to the ruling party. The collector's phone rang soon after and it was no less than the chief minister who asked for an explanation. 'Get him out at the soonest,' the collector was told. But when officials of the same district caught hold of a local BJD leader and put him behind bars a year later, no calls or messages came from the chief minister's office.

Odisha was witnessing change after a long time and even the state secretariat, the seat of power, seemed sanitized. Gone were the shady-looking characters who roamed the corridors during previous regimes. Ministers and ruling partymen were also more circumspect, knowing that the new chief minister would not cover up any of their misdeeds. It wasn't as if corruption had been swept away totally, but outwardly at least it wasn't all-pervasive as it used to be.

Those used to throwing their weight around, including an additional director general of police (ADG), realized their powers had been curtailed. The ADG had a long-running dispute with some neighbours in his ancestral village and one day he visited the village to threaten them. He beat up a few villagers and warned them of dire consequences if they didn't fall in line. The story made it to the local press and subsequently to the new chief minister's office. 'Lock him up if he does not stop,' Naveen instructed the director general of police. The ADG did not visit his village after that.

Then there was the case of the Khariar royal family in western Odisha, with two of their members accused of abusing an eight-year-old domestic worker. As Prasanta Nahak lay in a hospital bed recovering from the brutalities he was subjected to allegedly by two royals, Bhubaneswar Singh Deo and his wife Pushpalata, the child's heart-breaking story made newspaper headlines. 'I was made to sit on a heater. It was hot,' Nahak said, recounting the torture he endured for minor transgressions at the Lal Mahal Palace. The alleged abuse dominated local news for days and Bhubaneswar Singh Deo, the son of a late state minister, was arrested. Like every other royal family, the Khariar royals were well networked and they sought help from their influential friends. Members of other royal families in Odisha, some of them prominent BJD leaders, sought to intervene and requested the chief minister for help. But Naveen dismissed them all, saying the crime committed did not justify any mercy. 'Let him rot,' Naveen retorted.

Though a man of few words, the chief minister had sent out a message, loud and clear, that he would brook no impropriety. It is debatable how proper some of his own political manoeuvrings were, but it was clear from the outset that Naveen wanted to play straight when it came to matters of governance. He seemed to genuinely care for those who needed help. He drew a salary as chief minister, but in the first few years of his term within minutes of the money being credited to his account the entire amount would be transferred to the bank account of the local SOS Children's Village which housed hundreds of orphans. He donated part of his salary to the needy without drawing attention to it.

Naveen also showed a compassionate side. When a fire ripped through a slum in Cuttack, some 25 kilometres from Bhubaneswar, and a Muslim tailor lost his house and belongings, Naveen immediately sent a car to fetch the Muslim family to the chief minister's office. The tailor said he needed around ₹1 lakh to rebuild his house and another ₹50,000 for the sewing machines he had lost. Money was promptly given from the Chief Minister's Relief Fund. It didn't end there. Six months later, an IAS officer was sent to check on the well-being of the family. By then, the tailor had turned into a die-hard Naveen follower. 'Till my last breath, I will be his,' he said, overflowing with gratitude.

A widow in Dasmantpur of Koraput district was equally grateful. The chief minister was visiting the southern district when the lady fell at his feet. A mother of two, she was pregnant with a third child, but her husband, a trucker, had died in a road accident two months earlier. The lady sobbed, seeking help, and Naveen was shaken. He got into the car to be driven to the helipad from where he would fly to another district, but kept repeating aloud, 'She is pregnant, has two children, her husband is dead. What will she do?' Officials in attendance attempted to reassure him that the lady would receive help from the district administration, but Naveen kept repeating, 'Pregnant, two children, dead husband. What will she do?' The seniormost bureaucrat accompanying the chief minister got the message. He called the collector and ordered that help should be provided straight away. An hour later, when Naveen disembarked from the helicopter he again asked the officials what the lady would do, and they told him the collector had already given her a widow pension, allotted her a house under the Indira Awaas Yojana and given her a job at the local anganwadi centre. Only then did the chief minister seem to relax.

~

Naveen's initial years in office weren't smooth sailing though. His political opponents tried everything within their means to spoil his name and dent his image. Soon after he assumed the office of chief minister for the first time, he got a taste of how low politics could descend.

One Biswanath Majhi of Panasaguda village of Kashipur block in Rayagada district had cooked a meal of rice and ragi for twenty-odd labourers he had hired to work in his field, in August 2001, but unfortunately four of them died after having the meal. His wife and one of his sons had eaten the same meal and also died. The deaths had the classic hallmarks of food poisoning. One of Majhi's sons survived since he had been at school and had not eaten the meal. But the media kicked up a huge storm, portraying these as starvation deaths, claiming that nineteen others had died of hunger in Rayagada in the previous month. The media refused to consider that the family members of Majhi, who had the financial means to hire labourers, could not have starved to death.

Media reports on hunger deaths and human deprivation were nothing new for Odisha. They had first begun in the mid 1980s, during J.B. Patnaik's tenure as chief minister, with the infamous Panas Punji–Banita case. (As mentioned earlier, Panas Punji of Kalahandi had reportedly sold her niece Banita to a blind man for ₹60 because she was unable to feed either herself or her niece.) The story shook the nation's conscience, and Prime Minister Rajiv Gandhi soon arrived in Kalahandi, along with his wife Sonia, and declared that he would adopt the district and pull it out of its wretched poverty.

Notwithstanding pledges made by the prime minister, Kalahandi and its adjoining regions – the erstwhile undivided districts of Balangir and Koraput – stubbornly remained poor and news of worsening conditions and growing hunger emerged periodically to embarrass whichever government was in power. Odisha had come to acquire the reputation of being a state where destitute children were sold for less than the price of a plate of chicken curry and the state's notoriety came to haunt Naveen very early in his tenure. At a press conference one evening in the state secretariat, soon after the Rayagada deaths, Naveen cut a sorry figure. Local journalists grilled him endlessly, hardly allowing him to speak. They aggressively held forth on why they were certain that the latest reports on hunger deaths in Rayagada district were true. New to the job, Naveen heard them attentively. 'Your government has failed,' said one irate journalist. 'You have blood on your hands,' quipped another. The mood in the conference hall was hostile as the local media railed against Naveen, accusing him of letting down the state.

Outside, the chief minister's rivals seemed to be even more aggressive. 'Who needs a government that cannot feed its own people?' asked J.B. Patnaik. The matter rocked Parliament in distant Delhi, where Congress chairperson Sonia Gandhi berated Naveen and his government for 'bad policy and bad management of the public distribution system'. Naveen's BJD was a partner of the ruling NDA and the mounting criticism over hunger deaths had put the Central government led by Prime Minister Atal Bihari Vajpayee in a spot. That the deaths would become fodder for the power-hungry politicians came as no surprise. While in power, the Congress led by J.B. Patnaik was regularly attacked by the opposition for letting hundreds die of hunger. The moment the Congress found itself in the opposition, it gleefully turned the tables on the ruling party by using starvation to its advantage. J.B. Patnaik had made a virtual career out of denying starvation deaths while he was the chief minister for fourteen years. As long as he was in power, he steadfastly maintained that no one died of hunger in Odisha. 'It is all politically motivated allegations,' he had invariably insisted. But as fresh allegations of hunger deaths hit the headlines and Naveen felt the heat, the wily politician, now out of power, smelt a chance and went all out to tar the reputation of the new chief minister.

The media dynamics in Odisha were such that journalists of national dailies and television channels readily provided support to the opposition. But for an occasional natural calamity or a rare VIP visit, Bhubaneswar-based journalists rarely had the opportunity to make headlines. Their reports were mostly used as fillers, buried in the day's news coverage of newspapers and television bulletins, and they carried little weight with their editors in Delhi. The only time the editors took note was when they came up with sensational stories of starvation deaths. Such reports were the sole means of establishing their relevance. As was the practice earlier, the media merrily reported more hunger deaths and the distress sale of children, factual or not, after the Rayagada story first broke.

There was no denying that Odisha was poor and that human distress was high in the state. But the hunger deaths that the media were citing didn't always pass scrutiny. Take for instance the case of Triveni Pidikaka of village Gajakupalli in Rayagada district who was reported to have died of starvation. Her death made it to prime-time television news, but a background check revealed that she earned ₹100 a month by cooking meals for children at a local school. The money she made was certainly a pittance, but it was inconceivable that someone cooking meals could die of hunger herself. The explanation by the district's chief medical officer that she probably died of chronic malaria or an underlying malignancy seemed more credible.

Media reports on starvation deaths had other glaring inconsistencies too. Some who were said to have died of starvation were found alive. Some others were found to have been repaying small loans they had taken from banks – you certainly don't repay loans and let yourself die of hunger.

One of the biggest stories reported around that time was that of the sale of two young children in Balangir in western Odisha. An intrepid reporter of *Hindustan Times* newspaper claimed to have bought the kids for a few hundred rupees. The family, it was said, was too poor to look after the children and was forced to sell them. Enquiries, though, revealed that the motive for the sale was more greed than distress. The children had lost their parents and their uncle handed them over to the reporter in exchange of cash, though the family had a balance of about ₹17,000 in the local cooperative bank account. They had also received a house under the Indira Awaas Yojana. By all accounts, the uncle was attempting to get rid of the kids whom he saw as an unnecessary burden – and also make a quick buck. Both the newspaper and the reporter made a huge fuss and claimed they would look after the children's well-being lifelong. But they went silent as the inconsistencies in the story gradually emerged. There has been no news of the two children since.

However, the media campaign against Naveen's 'incompetence' and 'indifference' was unrelenting. Adding to the embarrassment were ill-timed and insensitive remarks of certain bureaucrats. When the media reported that tribals in Odisha's interiors were forced to eat mango kernels in the absence of proper food and they were, consequently, dying in large numbers, an incredulous official asked, 'Who ate the mangoes then?' Another senior bureaucrat suggested that the kernels were a tribal staple. As the nation vented its outrage and a din of collective disapproval followed, details were overlooked or wilfully ignored.

Ironically, the media blitz on starvation provided little succour to the poor. Banita, the Kalahandi girl sold to the blind man in the 1980s for ₹60, epitomized the futility of the media coverage. Some ten years after the nationwide furore her sale had triggered, she was found to be living with the same man. She had by then borne three of his children, but she still lived as a social outcaste in her village. The local custom mandated that the couple host a feast for their marriage to be sanctioned. But Banita and her husband were too poor to pay for one. They were finally married in the year 2000 when Bhakta Charan Das, a former union minister, volunteered to foot the bill for the feast.

To a large extent, the media's unrelenting coverage of 'starvation deaths' was farcical. An editorial in a prominent Odia daily argued that even those who die after being knocked down by a speeding vehicle while crossing the road in the poverty-stricken districts of the state should be counted as victims of starvation deaths as years of malnutrition had robbed them of the ability to cross the road swiftly and with alacrity.

Naveen stopped holding press conferences after the noisy and raucous one at the state secretariat. The local media's hunger to pillory him put him off. It upset the local media, but they could do nothing about it. Since most outlets were owned by politicians, they lacked credibility and their ability to do real damage was limited. The chief minister's public persona, meanwhile, only endeared him to his people.

Naveen wasn't speaking Odia still, but his softer side was doing the talking, loud and clear. As and when he wanted to, he impressed people, including visiting dignitaries such as the head of the World Bank team. Odisha, in a financial mess then, was seeking to get foreign money assistance and the World Bank team was in India. Naveen's aides made him agree to host a private breakfast for the head. Initially reluctant, Naveen agreed, and the two headed for breakfast at a five-star hotel in Delhi. Post breakfast, the dignitary could not stop talking about the face-time he had with Naveen. More than the food, Naveen had impressed him with his deep knowledge about the history of Ireland – the country the World Bank team head hailed from. The loan took no time in coming. By the time the next assembly elections were held in 2004 – the polls were advanced by a year to be conducted simultaneously with Lok Sabha elections – his charm and charisma had only grown. That he had provided a cleaner government than the previous scandal-tainted Congress governments also helped immensely. Unlike many of the preceding chief ministers of Odisha, Naveen remained largely untarnished, though some of his partymen had courted controversies.

In the run-up to the elections, Naveen launched a charm offensive. His staff had drawn up a list of thousands of people – teachers, lawyers, doctors and others – who they thought were locally influential in the interiors of the state. The phone numbers of these influential men and women had been meticulously collected. Every evening ahead of the elections, for about two hours daily, the staff would dial the numbers one by one and Naveen would come to the phone. '*Namaskar, mu Naveen Patnaik kahuchhi. Kemiti acchanti? Shankha chinha re vote debe*' (Namaskar, I am

Naveen Patnaik speaking. How are you? Please vote for the conch symbol.), the chief minister would say, repeating the same rehearsed lines every time. The response at the other end was also repetitive. Stunned momentarily to hear from the chief minister, those receiving the calls were more often than not overjoyed.

Each call did not last more than a minute, but its effect lasted long. Naveen had brought in a personal touch to the political campaign under way, and the state once again reposed its faith in him. The BJD–BJP combine won handsomely: the BJD won 61 seats and the BJP 32. Together, they were well past the majority. The Congress won only 38 seats, having contested 133 of the total 147 seats. Naveen was the chief minister again.

~

Election campaigns are an expensive affair and the BJD spent extravagantly to win the 2004 vote. Leaders hopped around in helicopters, huge rallies were held and posters and placards plastered the state. Where did the money come from? Who gave the money? And why did they give money? Like every other political party in the country, Naveen's BJD is reticent about the funds they collect to run the party and its campaigns, with only a small coterie being privy to the information. Every political party furnishes expense statements to the Election Commission, but it is no secret that they are grossly understated.

There is nothing to suggest that the BJD is an exception. Being in power is the party's ultimate objective. Having wrested power in 2000, it wanted to renew its hold on power in 2004 and spent money lavishly to that end. Political pundits say it outspent the opposition by several times. If the Congress staged one rally at a place, the BJD held three rallies that were much bigger in size, scale and splendour.

Details are sketchy but what emerges is that, like every other party, the BJD too raises money from corporates, contractors and whoever is willing to contribute. The fund from where the party spends and which is constantly replenished with fresh donations is parked with one particularly trustworthy party functionary. Top party leaders call him the 'lifeline'. As and when money is needed, the 'lifeline' steps in. The BJD's first 'lifeline' was a retired bureaucrat who wielded tremendous influence over Naveen before they bitterly fell out. He is now dead. The new 'lifeline' is supposedly someone with strong connections with both corporates and Delhi.

But those in the know say Naveen's fund-raising activity is different from that of other political parties. While accepting donations, Naveen took extra care to retain his image of a clean, corruption-free administrator who valued probity, decency and decorum in public life. His BJD collected money, but the government that Naveen ran was not extortionist in the initial few years for sure. 'At least in the first two terms of his rule, there was no quid pro quo,' says a top aide. Donors were more than welcome to donate to the party fund, but they could not expect any favours in return. 'Naveen insisted there will be no sweet deals. He had zero tolerance towards corruption at the top level that could besmirch his own reputation,' the aide added. But donors still came forward and donated. Some work that the donors wanted done would get done in the normal course and they would be happy. Other donors would be happy earning the goodwill of the chief minister and his party, no mean capital in the world of business.

The aide cited the example of a businessman, the owner of a giant mining firm. He paid an annual tax of ₹500 crore and wanted to donate ₹5 crore to the party fund. The amount was small change for the rich miner. The donation perhaps got him no immediate benefits, but it gave him access to the ruling party. As and when he needed, he could call up ministers who would readily come on the line. Access to the chief minister's office also got easier. Word spread that the miner had access to people in high places and bureaucrats became nicer to him. Given the myriad benefits political donations bring, his investment wasn't a waste at all.

Backed by two rounds of resounding mandates, Naveen got down to the business of ruling Odisha with renewed vigour. The arrangement he had in place in the second term was a continuation of the one in his first stint. Pyari Mohapatra was all-powerful and continued to call the shots from his home at 111 Saheed Nagar, while many continued to believe that Naveen was still a learner. Only a few at the top level of the bureaucracy knew that the chief minister was calling the shots.

Take for instance the case of Lakshmanananda Saraswati, an octogenarian Hindu priest, who had come to live in Kandhamal in the 1960s. He was one of the two priests sent to the region by Hindu religious leaders of Puri, in a bid to stem what they saw as the ever-growing influence of Christian missionaries and to stop their proselytizing campaign. In a way, Kandhamal was a laboratory for Hindu hardliners who were looking for ways to widen their sphere of influence and Lakshmanananda Saraswati set about the task in right earnest, setting up Sanskrit schools and embarking on an aggressive drive to reconvert tribals who had converted to Christianity.

His area of activity in Kandhamal spread in an arc from Chakapada, bordering the district of Ganjam, to Tumudibandha on the edge of Kalahandi, and his stature grew in proportion to the many temples and schools he set up. He also built about a thousand sankirtan mandals – places where Hindus could come together to pray and sing hymns – and enjoyed complete control over about 40,000 people in the region.

On 23 August 2008 Lakshmanananda Saraswati was assassinated at his ashram – armed men barged into the ashram and opened fire. The motive for the murder remains a mystery. Some believe local Maoists carried out the hit at the behest of Christian leaders, who saw Lakshmanananda Saraswati as a threat. The Maoists reportedly agreed to carry out the killing to gain support among local Christians, who accounted for nearly 25 per cent of the region's population. Such support was crucial as the area was the gateway to neighbouring Chhattisgarh, where the Maoists escaped to whenever the police came after them. As news of the killing spread, Saraswati's followers went on a rampage, targeting those the priest had tirelessly worked against – the Christians. The month-long violence left at least fifty people dead and hundreds of homes and churches destroyed. While local officials were unanimous that the mayhem was not pre-planned or organized, many were queasy that the

BJP, associated with right-wing Hindu politics, was an ally of the chief minister's BJD. Saraswati belonged to the BJP-affiliated Vishwa Hindu Parishad (VHP), but the angry mob did not necessarily belong to any organization. Authorities insisted the VHP, and the BJP, had an organizationally limited role to play in the riots that swept Kandhamal.

Naveen wished to visit Saraswati's ashram and pay tribute to him, much to the surprise of his bureaucrats. 'Did not an old man die?' he sternly asked the startled officers, a rare moment when he lost his cool. The officials advised the chief minister to stay away from Saraswati's Jalespeta ashram. The last thing they wanted was for the chief minister to be photographed laying wreaths to a man many considered a religious zealot. Naveen too understood the political pitfalls. He realized that rivals could attribute motives to his visit and accuse him of siding with communal forces. Yet he threw caution to the winds and insisted on visiting the ashram. 'An old man has been killed and I will go to pay my respects. Let there be media photographers. It doesn't matter,' he said.

The officials were disappointed, but they deferred to his wishes. As the chief minister travelled to Jalespeta, undeterred by the presence of press photographers and television crews, people saw another facet of Naveen's complex character. As a practising politician, he was wily, shrewd, calculating and clinically cold. He could destroy rivals without batting an eyelid and betraying any emotion. But his humane side was once again on display – he seemed to be genuinely moved by the murder of the old priest.

Homage paid to the slain seer, Naveen was back to hatching his next political move. This time his coalition partner, the BJP, was in his crosshairs. The two parties had needed each other in the initial years and were closely associated since the time the BJD was formed. The BJP, as mentioned earlier, is believed to have bankrolled the nascent BJD to an extent. But after some eight years in power in the state as coalition partners – they ruled on a 4:3 ratio on seat sharing, with the BJD contesting 84 seats and the BJP 63 of the total 147 assembly seats – Naveen seemed to increasingly feel he no longer needed the BJP. Pyari Mohapatra, his principal adviser, shared his belief, having already floated several trial balloons to test the mood even before Lakshmanananda Saraswati's assassination and the Kandhamal riots that followed.

In 2008, the BJD appointed a private agency to gauge the political mood in the state and was startled by the feedback. The report said that the importance given to the BJP in the BJD–BJP coalition was disproportionate to the saffron party's actual strength with the electorate and that it was winning assembly seats mostly by piggy-backing on the BJD. The findings emboldened the BJD to fight the municipal elections solo in the central Odisha town of Anugul, pitting candidates against both the Congress and the BJP. The gamble paid off and the BJD improved its tally by almost 40 per cent. Another opportunity to test the party's strength came in November that year, when local body elections were held in Bhubaneswar. The BJD went to the polls without the BJP and won 39 of the 60 seats. It bettered its record in the local body elections in Cuttack in February 2009, winning 36 of the 54 seats on its own merit. Now all Naveen needed was an opportune moment to sever ties with the BJP and that came with the April 2009 assembly elections. Always looking to consolidate power, he blamed the Kandhamal riots on the alliance partner and announced what he had been planning silently for a long time – a political divorce with the BJP.

Naveen allegedly tried to cut his ally down to size by offering the BJP far fewer assembly and Lok Sabha seats to contest from – only 31 assembly seats though the saffron party had 32 MLAs in the outgoing assembly and 5 parliamentary seats against 7 sitting BJP MPs.

The BJP was obviously aghast at what it saw as Naveen's 'betrayal'. The party tried its best to salvage its alliance and sent emissaries such as the journalist and former MP Chandan Mitra to negotiate with Naveen. The chief minister, as always, was courteous to Mitra when he visited him at his home. But he stood his ground and the BJD–BJP coalition that had yielded tremendous electoral dividends in the past collapsed.

But few shed tears for the BJP. Overwhelmed by the power that they had come to enjoy for the first time in their careers, BJP ministers and legislators competed with one another to be unpopular. Most of them were known to be inefficient and dishonest and when Naveen dumped them no one in the state really missed them. The party fulminated for a while, promising to wreak vengeance on Naveen and teach him a lesson he wouldn't easily forget. But without a party structure and mass base, these were just empty threats.

When the 2009 assembly results were declared, it was Naveen and his BJD alone that had reasons to cheer. The BJP had no place to hide, having won just 6 of the 145 assembly seats it contested. Naveen's party won 103 seats while the Congress won 27. Naveen thus became chief minister for the third time. While the BJP's contribution to the formation of the BJD could never be forgotten, by 2009, Naveen did not need it and the party joined the long list of those he had used and thrown aside, a list that was soon to get longer.

Chief minister since 2000, Naveen was finally coming into his own. He could still not converse in Odia, but had begun to understand the language that his partymen and his people spoke. He understood the politics as well as the pulls and pressures that were at play in the state. He had grown familiar with the leaders and party workers and also the places they came from. He felt comfortable in his role as the state's top elected representative. But one irritant remained: Pyari Mohapatra. Having helped Naveen find his feet and tighten his hold over the state, the adviser had assumed a larger-than-life profile. He became a staple of hushed conversations among ordinary people, and politicians speculated about his contribution to building Brand Naveen. Much of what was said was not very flattering to the chief minister. Many believed Pyari Mohapatra was Naveen's brains and was the principal architect behind the chief minister's achievements. It was commonly believed that Naveen was a 'political pygmy' riding to success on Pyari Mohapatra's political acumen. But the 'pygmy' thought differently and the problems, in what was originally thought to be a protégé–mentor relationship, soon began bubbling up.

'I realized I was in a problem when Naveen came to see me off one day and opened the door of my car,' Pyari Mohapatra recounted some years later to me.

Having mentored him for close to a decade, Pyari Mohapatra believed he had a good measure of how Naveen's mind worked. 'If Naveen is being extra nice, then you are in a spot,' Pyari Mohapatra elaborated, talking about the dinner meeting that he had in Naveen Niwas sometime in 2010. Not content with being just a back-room adviser, Pyari Mohapatra had taken on a much larger public role. He had become a BJD-nominated Rajya Sabha member for the first time in 2004 and was now sharing the public stage with Naveen. During the 2009 elections, he went out to campaign for the party, taking off in a separate helicopter as Naveen flew in another.

But once the dust of electioneering settled and Naveen was firmly back in the chief minister's chair, Pyari Mohapatra's stock began to gradually decline. At first, it wasn't obvious at all. Naveen, who always came across as decent, was still deferential to Pyari Mohapatra, who had once been his father's aide. In public, he would always stand up when the former bureaucrat made his entry. Or he would tell his staff to check with Pyari Babu before signing off a crucial administrative decision. But in private, a degree of coldness crept in and Pyari Mohapatra suspected it all began when Gita Mehta, Naveen's sister, made an impromptu suggestion one evening in 2010 in the presence of the chief minister. Increasingly worried about her brother's health and his long hours of work, Gita suggested that Pyari Mohapatra should be made deputy chief minister to lessen the chief minister's burden. Naveen kept quiet but Pyari Mohapatra says it must have set the alarm bells ringing. 'He must have thought that if his sister felt that way, many partymen could also be thinking likewise – seeing me as someone very capable of running the state,' Pyari Mohapatra told me.

The dinner over, Naveen came to see him off and opened the car door for Pyari Mohapatra. 'He opened the car door and then shut the door of the party on me,' Pyari Mohapatra said.

For a while, the relationship between the mentor and protégé continued and both went about their business. But suspicion had started creeping in and shook the trust that bound them together. In 2011, Pyari Mohapatra strategized and campaigned hard and the BJD won the assembly by-election for Umerkote in the far-flung Nabarangpur district. Since he was the principal architect of the BJD poll strategy, Naveen routinely thanked Pyari Mohapatra after every election victory. Strangely though this time, the chief minister did not congratulate him. On the rare occasions they met, the chief minister politely suggested that Mohapatra, already seventy-one years old, should take care of his health and refrain from whirlwind campaigns by criss-crossing the state in a helicopter. But Pyari Mohapatra failed to take the hint and kept the same hectic political pace, refusing to step away from the spotlight.

During the zilla parishad elections of early 2012, a headstrong Pyari Mohapatra waded into a bigger controversy as he hit the campaign trail again. At election rally venues in places like Soran in Khordha district, giant cut-outs of Pyari Mohapatra towered over those of Naveen. Mohapatra insisted he had not instructed party workers to put them up and claimed he did not know who was behind them. But Naveen got them publicly pulled down. The chief minister said little, but had unmistakably begun to cut Pyari Mohapatra down to size. In between, when Mohapatra went to Berhampur in Ganjam on personal work, his request to be given a room for a few hours to rest at the Circuit House was turned down by district officials. Till then, Pyari Mohapatra's word had been law. But in the changed circumstances, he could not even get a room for himself in the Circuit House.

The obvious slights kept piling up. The phone calls from the chief minister dried up completely and contact between the two stopped. It stayed that way for some months till Pyari Mohapatra could bear it no longer. Feeling insulted and ignored, Pyari Mohapatra got progressively angrier.

The former bureaucrat had played a key role in the 2009 assembly elections and had virtually hand-picked most of the BJD party candidates. Convinced that many of the elected legislators were his men and would stay loyal to him, Pyari Mohapatra called for a meeting of the MLAs at his home on 29 May 2012. 'I was upset and just wanted to show I still had influence,' he explained. But as some three dozen MLAs trooped in for the meeting, the Naveen camp struck. The chief minister was on a trip to the United Kingdom to court foreign investors, his first foreign visit as the chief minister after twelve years in power. Some local television channels, led by one owned by a party MP close to Naveen, built up a breathless narrative, saying a coup plot was under way in Saheed Nagar.

All hell broke loose and other BJD leaders and legislators rushed to Naveen Niwas in a show of solidarity for the chief minister. Pyari Mohapatra kept protesting, saying he neither had the intention nor the means to topple Naveen. 'With thirty MLAs, you cannot unseat a chief minister,' he insisted. He had booked the banquet hall and several rooms of a city luxury hotel for the legislators, but had not sought any appointment with the Governor, something he would have had to do if he had wanted to stake a claim to the chief minister's chair. 'All the talk of a coup was misplaced and false,' Pyari Mohapatra said. But amid the din of the attempted coup with television channels broadcasting live from the front of his house, Pyari Mohapatra's protestations found no takers. It was Odisha's NTR moment, a throwback to the emotive events of 1984 when a Telugu Desam insider, N. Bhaskara Rao, sought to usurp the chair of then Andhra Pradesh chief minister N.T. Rama Rao. Like Naveen, NTR too had been out of the country, but for medical treatment of serious ailments, when Bhaskara Rao staged his coup and became the chief minister. Taken by surprise, an ailing Rama Rao hastened back to the state in a wheelchair and claimed he had been wronged. Swayed by the images of a wheelchair-bound NTR pleading for justice, people hit the streets in large numbers across the state in his support and Bhaskara Rao's mutiny proved short-lived. Rama Rao reclaimed the chief minister's chair, riding a sympathy wave.

Naveen, too, hurried back to Odisha and his return two days later was as poignant and dramatic. Thousands of party workers thronged Bhubaneswar airport to receive him as Naveen projected the image of being wronged by a man he trusted. He was driven to his home in a huge procession and leaders and legislators alike competed with one another to prove their loyalty to him. Never a man of the masses, Pyari

Mohapatra lost the narrative and control of the party. Naveen did not have to say much to turn the tables on his one-time mentor. As journalists pressed him about the attempted plot to unseat him, he said it was the work of a 'beimaan' (cheat). A terse statement followed, saying Pyari Mohapatra had been suspended from the party. Disciplinary action also followed against several of the legislators considered loyal to the fallen leader.

In all probability, Pyari Mohapatra was sabre-rattling and seeking to flex his muscles by gathering the MLAs loyal to him. He missed his proximity to Naveen and the attendant powers that came with it and was desperate to grab the chief minister's attention by whichever means. But once described as the Chanakya of Odisha politics, he was outsmarted by Naveen. Helped by friendly television channels, the chief minister and his camp reportedly sold the narrative that Pyari Mohapatra was out to stab Naveen in the back and seized the opportunity to do away with him. Once Pyari Mohapatra was projected as a villain, the rest was easy. As with previous instances of rivals being shown the door, Pyari Mohapatra's exit helped Naveen emerge stronger.

Pyari Mohapatra kept insisting till he died some years later that he had never attempted to stage a coup. But Naveen and his men insisted there had indeed been an attempt. Like the rest of Naveen's rivals who were no match for his guile, Pyari Mohapatra too cut a sorry and lonely figure. The queues before his house quickly evaporated and both politicians and bureaucrats who had cowered before him now took extra precautions not to be seen anywhere near him. For some time, Pyari Mohapatra kept up his bluster, threatening to expose the chief minister. He formed a political outfit, the Odisha Jan Morcha, and contested the polls, but failed to make a dent. None of his candidates came close to winning and the outfit was a non-starter. His political obituary was written long before he died at a Mumbai hospital in March 2017. When his body arrived in Odisha, Naveen was one of the first to pay his respects at Bhubaneswar airport.

With Pyari Mohapatra, his mentor, no more by his side, many began to believe Naveen's days were numbered as well. 'The brain gone, how long can the body survive,' said a Congress leader gleefully, still believing that Naveen was politically naive. Many clung on to the belief that Naveen wasn't capable of surviving the minefield of politics on his own, such was the smoke and mirrors illusion of innocence and naivety that Naveen had managed to maintain. They were proven wrong when in two years, in 2014, Odisha voted in parliamentary and state assembly elections simultaneously amid a Modi hawa. The Gujarat chief minister Narendra Modi was the prime ministerial candidate of the BJP-led NDA and an upsurge of support for him began to grow strongly across the country. Odisha was not an exception. Modi promised to change India, end corruption and provide jobs. His fluent, rousing oratory found ready takers in Odisha and elsewhere. His rallies in the state drew huge, exuberant crowds and the turnouts had observers predicting that voters of the state were finally ready to desert Naveen.

Fourteen years in power is a long time and those in the opposition felt Naveen's novelty had worn off. He had won the first election in 2000 riding a sympathy wave for his late father. That wave had long ceased to exist and the subsequent elections were won by Naveen on the strength of his own image and the changes he had brought about in the state administration. A disorganized and virtually non-existent opposition also helped his cause. Now that his image was pitted against the mightier image of Modi, there were many who felt that Naveen may have finally met his match. As the poll bugle was sounded and high-voltage electioneering got under way, political pundits began writing the political obituary of the chief minister.

But amid the raucous electioneering and the unruly rallies, most pundits failed to notice the finer political nuances. The crowds that Modi attracted were mostly members of the more vociferous urban middle classes. Educated youths outnumbered the rest in Modi rallies. Naveen's rallies, in comparison, were staid and much smaller. Not known to be a speaker who could light up the river Mahanadi with his oratory, Naveen mostly stuck to reading out Odia speeches written for him in roman script in his gruff voice. His rallies were lacklustre and there was little to write home about. His audience looked much poorer and less urban than those who invariably turned up for Modi rallies. The crowds that Naveen attracted were silent and stoic compared to their urban counterparts. But in them lay the unmistakable signs of things to come.

The Modi wave swept large tracts of the country and the BJP-led NDA won state after state, bagging more than 300 Lok Sabha seats. But when it came to Odisha, it came a cropper. When the results of the Lok Sabha and assembly elections were announced in the state, Naveen, it emerged, had not only weathered the Modi storm but had also beaten it back conclusively. Out of the 21 Odisha Lok Sabha seats, his BJD had won 20. The BJP won just one. The results of the assembly elections were no less astounding and left pundits scratching their heads in disbelief. Bucking the trend of anti-incumbency, the ruling BJD bettered its tally. Compared to 103 seats it won in 2009, this time the party won 117 of the total 147 seats. The Congress won 16 and the BJP, despite riding the Modi wave, got just 10.

Never given to showing emotions, Naveen returned to his official chambers on the third floor of the state secretariat in Bhubaneswar the day after the 2014 results were announced, without fanfare. He had a habit of not coming to the office once election dates were announced and until he was re-elected. Once he returned in 2014, partymen and officials lined up to congratulate him, but the chief minister reminded them that there was little time to celebrate. 'We have a larger mandate and therefore a bigger responsibility. Please get back to work,' he told his closest aides.

The 2014 election results solidified Naveen's position as a political giant. Having outwitted and outsmarted all his rivals, Naveen was king of all he surveyed. There was no one in the party who could match up to his stature or charisma. Naveen did not need his partymen. They needed him for their own political survival. Partymen and officials feared him. Over the years Naveen had built a formidable reputation of being what a Bhubaneswar-based political commentator, Rabi Das, calls a 'smiling assassin'. Post-2014, no one was left within the ruling party who could challenge Naveen in any way. The party was emaciated from within, with almost all the big leaders neutralized. And it was Naveen alone who mattered in Odisha.

~

Naveen's writ now ran large and it wasn't exactly a good idea to run afoul of it. Prakash Mishra, considered an honest and upright officer of the Indian Police Service (IPS), found that out the hard way after becoming Odisha's director general of police (DGP).

A 1977-batch officer, Mishra's impeccable integrity was well known and Naveen was impressed. He appointed Mishra DGP in 2012 and was happy with his work. Several southern districts of Odisha such as Rayagada, Malkangiri and Koraput were Maoist hotbeds and Mishra did a commendable job in retrieving lost ground for the administration. His men fought long and hard and pushed the insurgents on the back foot. Several top Maoists surrendered while the majority retreated into the adjoining states of Chhattisgarh and Andhra Pradesh. Mishra took his job seriously and in the run-up to the 2014 elections, his force even seized several ambulances that were reportedly ferrying unaccounted campaign cash for the ruling BJD. The seizures made news and Mishra began to feel the heat in the middle of the high-decibel electioneering. 'I was told my actions will be watched,' Mishra recounted.

Elections over, he was keen on a central deputation where he was eyeing the coveted position of director of the Central Bureau of Investigation (CBI) that was to fall vacant after the retirement of the incumbent Ranjit Sinha. He was the seniormost among those in the race and the department of personnel and training also had him on the top of its list. But the Odisha government was dilly-dallying on Mishra's release – an officer working for a state government has to be 'released' by the state before he can go to work at the Centre. So much so that the union home minister Rajnath Singh reportedly had to intervene to get the Odisha government to relieve Mishra so that he could take over as special secretary in the ministry of home affairs in Delhi. The selection for the post of CBI director was to be made in December 2014, and Mishra's name was commonly cited in the media as the most likely choice.

But sometime in October, Mishra got mired in a controversy that blew his chances of heading the CBI. The vigilance department of the Odisha government, under orders of the chief minister, dug up some old files relating to his stint as the chairman and managing director of the Odisha Police Housing Corporation in 2006 and registered a case against him for alleged misappropriation of money. The case was flimsy. Mishra was accused of paying advances to companies for material to be procured – a standard practice in state bodies – and irregularities to the tune of about ₹70 lakh. The complaint registered failed to identify who Mishra had benefited or whether anyone benefited at all. It also did not take note of the fact that the material for which advance payments were made was indeed procured.

The case against Mishra made national news. Mishra challenged it before the Odisha High Court and the judges handed a stinging rebuke to the Odisha government. But it took months before he could get a clean chit and by that time his claim for the CBI top job had been overlooked. 'The case filed by Naveen Patnaik against me ruined my chances. It was plain and simple vendetta,' Mishra was to accuse later. Having missed the CBI job, he became head of the Central Reserve Police Force (CRPF). But leading the paramilitary CRPF was not the same as heading the high-profile CBI and Mishra remains a bitter man. But why did he become subject of the wrath of the Odisha government?

Other than the seizure of the ambulances carrying cash, there has been speculation that Mishra, as DGP, had tried to help the BJP, thereby earning the displeasure of the chief minister. It is something that Mishra strongly denies. He, however, says that as a citizen of the country he believed that the BJP under

Modi would be doing very well in the elections and he routinely discussed such election-related matters with friends. He suspects that one such conversation was recorded by his professional rivals in the police force and was sent to the chief minister. In Odisha, this sort of medieval court espionage isn't too far-fetched. This allegedly enraged Naveen and he did everything within his power to destroy Mishra. Aides and associates who vouched for Mishra's integrity attempted to intervene and calm down the infuriated chief minister, but attempts at reconciliation failed.

The high court's order in June 2015 was a stinging indictment of the way in which the Odisha government had conducted itself. 'It is not very uncommon in our country that honest and upright public servants with unimpeachable integrity and having impeccable track record are often hounded by the ruling political establishment for extraneous consideration. In the present case, what is more disturbing is that the Director, Vigilance, to whom the file was marked by the chief minister for conducting an enquiry, has abdicated his duty and responsibility. The action or the rather wilful inaction of the Director, Vigilance, in not ensuring free, fair and proper enquiry into the matter and allowing the report of a sham enquiry to be accepted and giving his consent for seeking approval of the state government for registration of criminal case against the petitioners clearly shows that he was more concerned in exhibiting his loyalty to the ruling political establishment, akin to the old British adage of more loyal than the king.'

The court was not done yet. It concluded: 'The FIR and the materials available in the case diary and even the purported incriminating materials pointed out by the learned counsel for the Vigilance Department . . . do not constitute or disclose commission of any cognisable offence.' The judges quashed the case against Mishra, saying, 'Continuance of criminal proceedings against the petitioner would be an abuse of the process of Court and result in serious miscarriage of justice.'

Mishra had his reputation restored, but the Odisha government still went after him. It challenged the order of the Odisha High Court and took the matter to the Supreme Court. This time, the government hired several of the country's most expensive lawyers such as Harish Salve and Abhishek Manu Singhvi to argue the case against Mishra. In attempting to fix Mishra, the state government burnt a big hole in its pocket. However, the top court dismissed its plea and the government ended up with egg on its face. The matter would have ended there and possibly been forgotten as a temporary blemish by an administration that prided itself on propriety had Naveen not chosen to pursue it further.

In displaying an almost 'I don't care attitude', Naveen now chose to reward the same discredited director of vigilance who had strongly been criticized by the high court. Naveen made K.B. Singh the director general of Odisha police in 2015, a position that the officer held until August 2017.

Though an unsavoury episode, this exposed a dark side of Naveen, hidden behind his Teflon-coated exterior. The people of Odisha, however, seem to remain enamoured with him.

How Naveen wins elections so consistently is as fascinating a story as that of Naveen himself.

4

The Secret of Naveen's Success

'After so many years, one must admit that Naveen Patnaik understands Odisha better than all of us.'

This could be the sentiment on the ground and of Naveen's partymen, but coming from Bijoy Mohapatra, nursing his bitterness for many years, the statement is a shocker. Elected three times as a member of Parliament, and five times as the chief minister, Naveen had been a political marvel with few parallels that even sworn political enemies have been forced to acknowledge.

Pawan Kumar Chamling of Sikkim had been the country's only chief minister who has had a longer stint in power than him. Chamling, founder of the Sikkim Democratic Front (SDF), had been in power in the hill state between 1994 and 2019 for 24 years and 165 days.

Having won the assembly elections in 2019, Naveen bettered the records of Manik Sarkar – the

Tripura chief minister between 1998 and 2018 – and that of Jyoti Basu, the West Bengal chief minister for 23 years between 1977 and 2000. He also surpassed the record of J.B. Patnaik, Odisha's most successful politician until Naveen appeared on the scene. J.B. Patnaik had ruled the state for some 14 years – from 1980 to 1989 and then from 1995 to 1999. But while J.B. Patnaik's long rule was periodically rocked by controversies, Naveen's innings had been significantly smooth and comparatively uneventful.

In the initial years after Naveen denied Mohapatra the election ticket at the last moment, he was filled with rage and was plotting revenge. Every now and then, the media-friendly Mohapatra would announce that the chief minister's days were numbered and that the people of Odisha had seen through the man. But in the many years that went by with Naveen firmly in the saddle, none of Mohapatra's predictions came true. The desire for revenge diminished over time, and Mohapatra now accepts that Naveen had outwitted seasoned politicians like him. The final capitulation though came ahead of the general elections of 2024. Running out of options and having failed to get re-elected ever, Mohapatra let his young son, Arabinda, join the BJD. Naveen, too, reciprocated, giving his erstwhile rival's son a party ticket, and Arabinda became an MLA.

Narsingha Mishra, once Biju Patnaik's law minister and currently a senior Congress leader, is also not hesitant to acknowledge Naveen's prowess. 'Yes, he had been very successful in winning election after election. That's a feat that any politician will be proud of and opponents jealous of,' he conceded.

So how did Naveen go about winning elections so regularly and with such seeming ease? What was the magic? What was the secret of his success? Why did Odias embrace so firmly a man who did not speak their language? And how did he manage not to succumb to anti-incumbency, which ought to have knocked out the shine of the man many years ago? Why was the faith of Odias in Naveen so total and so overwhelming despite his trademark aloofness? Though he communicated barely with the people, how was it that their bond had been so strong and so long-lasting?

~

'Naveen won big because he was primarily a minimalist,' said a top bureaucrat who had in the past been a close associate of his. Ever since Naveen first campaigned to be elected as the MP from Aska, hiding his lit cigarette from the people, he had been mindful of his image. Unlike the other average politicians of Odisha, synonymous with pompousness and hubris, Naveen stayed low-key and shy. He came without baggage. He uprooted himself from his cocktail circuit and came to live in Bhubaneswar, without family or friends. In the initial years, he only had two acquaintances to share a drink with at Naveen Niwas – A.U. Singh Deo and Jay Panda. But despite being the most powerful person in the state, his social circle only shrunk. Despite determining the destiny of 4.5 crore Odias, he mostly drank whisky alone at home, after having distanced himself from both Singh Deo and Panda. But for an IAS officer – his private secretary – who in later years became his constant shadow, Naveen made no new friends. He generally kept to himself and his spartan lifestyle – *kurta-pyjama* and *chappals* without any ostentatious outward sign – and thus left little room for accusations to be levelled at him.

That he had no family or friends hanging about immensely helped Naveen to bolster his image as incorruptible. From time to time, his ministerial colleagues and party legislators got embroiled in controversies. They intermittently faced accusations of making money or helping cronies make money. But Naveen was generally spared such accusations. 'Why would he be corrupt? Without family, he had no reasons to be corrupt,' pointed out Anjali Behera, a housewife in the coastal town of Kendrapara. Such sentiments were commonly shared, both in the state's urban centres and in its rural heartland. 'Naveen Babu was never corrupt, though his men might have been,' insisted Trilochan Bhoi, a part-time teacher in the tribal district of Keonjhar. That Naveen was personally honest was a widely held belief that survived the test of time. Even political rivals conceded that accusations of corruption at a personal level did not stick or tarnish Naveen. Rabi Das, a political commentator, was never a fan of Naveen. Yet, he readily acknowledged that his integrity was never in doubt. 'Why would he need to be dishonest? He had no reasons to be,' explained Das. Prasad Harichandan was the Odisha Congress president from 2014 to early 2018. Even he confessed that targeting Naveen over graft was a difficult task. 'He was always seen to be honest. You may call it our failure,' Harichandan admitted.

Those who worked with Naveen insist his minimal personal needs resonated with the voters and sustained his honest image. 'Apart from cigarettes, his daily quota of drinks and maybe the power that came along with the position of chief minister, there was nothing else that possibly attracted him,' said one of them. He dressed simply, ate sparingly, smoked heavily and drank leisurely.

Naveen always had a simple way of looking at life, his journalist friend Vir Sanghvi wrote, recounting the chief minister's earlier years in a weekly pullout of the *Hindustan Times* a decade ago. 'Pappu [Naveen's pet name] didn't seem at all concerned about worldly goods. He lived at the right address, had two servants and a car and a driver [he can't drive], but that was about it. He never ate at fancy restaurants, and guests to his house, no matter how grand, ate whatever Manoj, the cook, made. His entire wardrobe seemed to consist of elegant but basic kurta-pyjamas.' Sanghvi went on to write that Naveen, when asked one day in a 'slightly drunken moment' about his simplicity, said, 'I have seen the most beautiful things in people's houses. To love beauty, you don't need to own it. You must just appreciate it.'

That being the guiding principle of Naveen's life, it is not hard to guess why Odias overwhelmingly fell for him and were convinced that he was Mr Clean. His somewhat clinical and detached behaviour helped in no small measure. When he came to live in Bhubaneswar, he did not bring his friends from Delhi. Some of them did stay in touch and visited Odisha occasionally, but Naveen generally kept them at arm's length. He met up and socialized with them a few times a year, but that was only when he visited Delhi and some of the old friends gathered discreetly at some hotel. Apparently, Naveen's friends from all over the world missed him. Hundreds of greeting cards sent by friends poured in every year on his birthday and the New Year. Some wrote long, intimate and personal messages. Some years ago, he got a message from a member of the royal family of Monaco. Naveen read the messages, but rarely replied. But why not? His take was simple: 'I am fine, they are fine. Why bother?'

His extended family also spared him the blushes. Naveen was closest to his sister Gita, but she lived with her family in the US. She visited often to check on her brother, but preferred to stay within Naveen Niwas, away from the public gaze. Prem lived in Delhi and rarely visited. One of the rare visits was when he, accompanied by his chief minister-brother, went to Cuttack to donate their ancestral house Anand Bhavan to the state. Naveen also did not seem particularly close to Prem's family either. Arun Patnaik, Prem's young, lanky son, was spotted during Prem's and Naveen's trip to Cuttack. It instantly triggered speculation that he could be at the core of the family's political succession plan. The boy went back and subsequently, the rumours ran out of steam.

Being alone helped Naveen immensely in a state where politicians in power were known to run a family empire. When J.B. Patnaik ruled, the fortunes of his family grew. Members of his extended family were always around, to the extent that if someone had to throw a stone in Odisha, the saying was, the stone would certainly hit a Patnaik. But Naveen turned out to be different.

That Naveen displayed no soft corner or attachment – at least for most part of his first few terms as the chief minister – was his biggest political asset. A top bureaucrat, who served him at the chief minister's secretariat and on whom Naveen depended heavily, had an interesting story to tell. The official's stint at the chief minister's office had come to an end and he was moving to another important assignment. The bureaucrat went to say goodbye to Naveen, but in going in and coming out of the chief minister's room, he barely took thirty seconds. Though known for courtesy and etiquette, Naveen refused to engage in any conversation. The officer was already a thing of the past in Naveen's mind and so, he felt no attachment to him any more. This trait of his explained his ability to sacrifice party colleagues and close associates so often. Given that he always showed people the door on the pretext of achieving something noble, he never attracted public disapproval. On the contrary, he was applauded for being decisive. And with every such 'decisive' action, Naveen's own image as a no-nonsense chief minister grew.

By rough estimates, Naveen showed the door to some eighty of his ministers during his five terms as the chief minister on some pretext or the other. It all began with the sudden axing of Nalinikanta Mohanty, who was also the working president of the party, along with two other ministers, Prashanta Nanda and Kamala Das. A year later, four more ministers – Debi Prasad Mishra, Amar Prasad Satpathy, Duryodhan Majhi and Adwait Prasad Singh – were sacked. Two of these were dropped on grounds of non-performance while the other two had to go due to alleged links to scams and corruption. They were followed by Pramila Mallik, the minister for women and child development, who had to step down a year later for not disclosing in her poll affidavit a case that was pending against her. In a nutshell, whenever there was the slightest whiff of a controversy, Naveen swiftly put the blame on someone else and removed them. He himself successfully came out unscathed.

Rabi Narayan Nanda was the high-profile minister for water resources and was caught in a sting in March 2006 that purportedly showed him attempting to buy the loyalty of an opposition MLA. All hell broke loose and Naveen acted with alacrity, sacking Nanda quickly. A hooch tragedy took place in Ganjam in April 2006 and excise minister Kalindi Behera had to go. Allegations of bribes engulfed a World

Bank–assisted health project in May the same year and health minister Bijayshree Routray had to put in his papers. Bishnu Charan Das, the school and mass education minister, faced accusations of having fudged his school-leaving examination mark sheet in August 2007. It embarrassed the government and Naveen forced Das to resign to save face. In all these cases, the underlying theme was the same – however high or mighty the person may be, Naveen would not tolerate their wrongdoings. Irrespective of their guilt or innocence, the ministers had to go and Naveen held on to people's trust.

Having first become the chief minister by virtue of being his father's son, Naveen never felt that he owed his position to any of his party colleagues. He, therefore, did not feel indebted to any of them. This tradition of his stood him in good stead, right until his final term when he was quixotically seen to have grown wholly dependent on his IAS secretary. But more of that later.

That caste equations or regional considerations – between coastal, central, western, northern and southern Odisha – never really played a determining role in electoral politics helped Naveen hugely. Naveen belonged to the Karana (Kayasth) caste, which accounted for less than 4 per cent of the state's population, but that was never a liability for him. Other backward classes (OBCs) and Chasas, or farmers, are the numerically dominant castes in Odisha. But while the state may be a bit conservative in matters of social life, with inter-caste marriages still frowned upon, castes have never been mobilized in a big way for electoral purposes and Odisha has had four chief ministers so far, out of a total of fourteen, from the numerically insignificant Karana caste. Interestingly, Odisha has also had a Bengali chief minister. Biren Mitra, who was the chief minister from 1963 to 1965, was a Bengali by birth though he and his parents had settled in Cuttack. Tensions do exist between coastal Odisha and western Odisha, with the latter accusing the former of cornering political power and government largesse, but the differences have never led to the regions voting differently. Instead, voters share a pan-Odisha identity, and this freed up Naveen from any caste and regional burdens.

Whenever someone got drawn into a scandal, Naveen's reflex action was to show them the door, irrespective of which caste or region they belonged to. So ministers continued to pay the price, one of the most prominent ones being the senior minister Damodar Raut, for his derogatory remarks against Brahmins. At a public function, Raut said, 'While no tribal is seen begging in any part of the state, one can spot brahmins resorting to begging in places such as bus stands.' His comment triggered an uproar and within days, Naveen sacked him from the council of ministers in December 2017.

Naveen generally did not allow any dirt to stick to him, no matter who was involved. Take, for instance, the case of a domestic discord between a young couple in Balasore that became a matter of public consternation in Odisha sometime in 2013. A young housewife alleged that her husband, the son of law minister and senior BJD leader Raghunath Mohanty, had been harassing her for dowry. Those in the dock were powerful people and public sympathy lay squarely with the housewife, the proverbial underdog. Unlike most other states where the administration would have sought to bail out the minister, Naveen's establishment did exactly the opposite. Raghunath Mohanty and his wife had gone underground and the police tracked them down. Cases were registered and the minister and his family members were arrested. Mohanty's standing in the public eye plunged, but Naveen's stock for standing up against any supposed wrongdoing rose exponentially. Some time later, the minister's son and his estranged wife patched up. But the minister never won back Naveen's favour, and his political career ended abruptly.

How much of Naveen's no-nonsense swiftness was because of personal conviction and how much due to political expediency remained a matter of speculation. On many occasions, having driven home the point that he would not tolerate any misconduct, Naveen went back to embracing the same set of people he had sacked for supposedly being tainted. 'He genuinely appreciated good things. But then he also had to dirty his hands from time to time to survive in politics,' said a bureaucrat who had seen Naveen operating from close quarters. 'Being a saint is not always good enough. One also has to be a Chanakya to succeed,' he added. Prashanta Nanda, the minister sacked alongside Nalinikanta Mohanty for being under the 'shadow of corruption' in 2001, and Maheswar Mohanty, the Odisha assembly speaker Naveen jettisoned in 2008 after he got embroiled in an alleged sex scandal involving a lady staffer, were among several politicians who managed to get back into Naveen's good books. They were given tickets to contest subsequent elections and were accommodated in various capacities once the controversies they were ensnared in died down. Nanda became a Rajya Sabha MP. Maheswar Mohanty became a minister later.

Several of the legislators axed for having sided with Pyari Mohan Mohapatra during the so-called coup in 2012 also found favour in later years. Prafulla Samal and Pratap Jena were two of them. Both became ministers when the alleged coup became a thing of the past.

Yet, the periodic surgeries that Naveen conducted, casting aside the local satraps, served a purpose. He determined the narrative and stayed above the scandals. It helped him sidestep public censure when a deadly fire ripped through a city hospital in Bhubaneswar and charred to death some twenty-four patients. Atanu Sabyasachi, the health minister, had to accept responsibility and step down to assuage public anger. Naveen, once again, escaped criticism, though, as the home minister, he too should have shared part of the blame. Administering the fire services department fell within the purview of the home minister and it later emerged that the fire safety audit of the Som Hospital had not been done for years.

~

Nurtured with care and aggressively shielded from wear and tear, Naveen's reputation helped him escape scrutiny when Odisha witnessed two of its largest scams in recent history – one related to mining and the other involving private firms running Ponzi schemes, popularly called chit funds. Despite his emphasis on providing a clean administration, the two extraordinarily organized plunders pushed the poor state and its people deeper into penury under Naveen's watch.

The mining scam involved an unbridled loot of the state's mineral resources which could, in size and scale, only be compared to the manner in which the more notorious Reddy brothers of Karnataka allegedly spirited away precious minerals worth thousands of crores from the mines in Bellary. The scandal happened when China was preparing to host the 2008 Beijing Olympics and its appetite for iron ore to boost steel production for building infrastructure was at its peak. Iron ore prices surged, from ₹1200 a tonne to ₹8000, and private players, virtually the who's who in the Indian corporate sector, sensed an easy killing. They plunged into mining iron ore and manganese from the tribal districts of Keonjhar and Sundargarh. In doing so, they either mined in excess of the limits set for them by various regulatory agencies or simply disregarded all norms and mined in areas without permission. The production of iron ore in Odisha rocketed – from 81 lakh tonnes in 1994–95 to 700 lakh tonnes in 2008–09. Exports stood at 163 lakh tonnes.

The Justice M.B. Shah Commission of Inquiry, which investigated the scam between 2010 and 2013, found that of the 192 mining leases of iron and/or manganese ores operating in Odisha during the mining boom, 147 lessees did not have proper agreements executed as per the Mines and Minerals

(Development and Regulation) – MMDR – Act 1957 which allows them to mine the land. As many as 94 did not have environmental clearances. Similarly, of the 176 leases located in forest areas, 47 mines operated without the necessary forest clearance from the ministry of environment and forests. The MMDR Act says that the monetary value of the illegal extraction is required to be recovered under Section 21(5) of the act. The Shah Commission pegged the scam to be worth ₹59,000 crore, while in August 2017 the Supreme Court asked the errant mining companies to pay ₹17,576 crore for excess extraction of iron ore and manganese.

Odisha led the iron ore boom in India, but got very little from it. This is because, in many cases, the ore was mined and sold, but not declared to the state government. Royalty on ore, which the state government got from mining, was very low. Between 2004 and 2012, a total of 5241.4 lakh tonnes of ore worth ₹199,847.5 crore was mined, but the royalty rates were between ₹8 and ₹27 per metric tonne, even though the price of ore rose to ₹8000. The Shah Commission was caustic in its findings, saying that the mine owners did not pay minimum wages to the labourers even though their own income was in crores. 'If the value of the iron ore and manganese mined in Sundargarh and Keonjhar districts for one year had been given to the tribal families of the two Odisha districts, each of the tribals would be richer by Rs 9.43 lakh. If the same amount was distributed among all the families of the two districts, they would be richer by Rs 4.5 lakh each,' the judge concluded.

The mining scam was the result of lax enforcement of rules and suspected nexus between mining firms and officials. A similar nexus was on display when the Ponzi schemes flourished in the state, defrauding tens of thousands of small depositors of their lifetime savings and threatening to besmirch the lily-white image of the chief minister.

Ponzi firms, which get their name from the Italian swindler Charles Ponzi, who defrauded thousands in the early twentieth century, collect money from investors by promising exorbitantly high returns. Old investors are repaid by money raised from new investors. This continues till the chain is broken when fresh investments dry up. While the initial investors have, by then, mostly got back their money, subsequent investors are left high and dry.

Dozens of Ponzi firms had a free run in Odisha, allegedly aided and abetted by influential politicians and their aides. Once the scam came to light and the CBI stepped in, several people were arrested and many others interrogated. One of those questioned was Saroj Sahu, an employee of Naveen Niwas who regularly issued BJD press releases under Naveen's name ahead of the 2014 elections. Several other leading politicians of the state were in the net. Among those jailed was Ramchandra Hansda, the BJD MP from Mayurbhanj and director of Nabadiganta Capital Services Limited, which fraudulently collected around ₹15 crore from investors and never bothered to return the money. BJD MLA Subarna Nayak and BJP MP Hitesh Bagarti were also arrested over links to the same company.

Others arrested included BJD MLAs Pravata Kumar Tripathy and Pravat Ranjan Biswal. Tripathy allegedly helped one Ranjan Kumar Das of Swastik India Multi State Credit Cooperative Society Limited. Das benefited from the state government. He raised money through recurring and retirement schemes in contravention of the law, but was rewarded with a nomination to the Odisha State Cooperative Council, the government body which makes policy decisions in the state cooperative sector. The nomination allowed him to gain in stature and thus benefit his business. Biswal, on the other hand, was in the dock for his alleged dubious land deal with the Seashore Group of Companies, whose owner faced thirty-nine criminal cases and who was also said to be involved in a Ponzi scheme.

It was a close shave for Naveen when it came to chit funds. He was seen gracing the 2011 launch of a news channel started by Seashore, whose owner later spent years in jail for involvement in the organized cheating. Twenty lakh investors in Odisha are believed to have been defrauded of about ₹5000 crore by Ponzi firms such as Seashore, but at the height of the fraud the Odisha government lent the Seashore group credibility by entering into a clutch of partnerships with it in sectors such as health, pharma, dairy and food processing. Each of the tie-ups flopped as Seashore lacked both the intent and the expertise, but it had a field day until the bubble burst and the CBI came knocking.

The twin scams shook the people's confidence in Naveen's government. But the criticism against Naveen as the chief minister was generally conspicuous by its absence. Asharani Panda, a housewife from Balasore, lost her life's saving to a Ponzi firm, lured by its attractive interest rates. As she rued her fate, she refrained from railing against Naveen. 'He was a good man, but all his men were crooks. It is they who ruined me,' she said. Prakash Senapati, a small-time trader in Koraput, lost around ₹1 lakh to a Ponzi firm, yet preferred to blame everyone else but Naveen. 'He was a nice man and did not maky money. But others in his team had huge appetites and could even swallow elephants,' he explained, gesturing with his hands to show how greedy the ruling party men were.

Those cheated by the chit funds formed associations and are still fighting legal battles for refunds. They accused the state of turning a blind eye to their plight, but few levelled charges of personal culpability against Naveen. For the overwhelming majority of those defrauded by the chit fund firms, Naveen's individual integrity was beyond reproach.

As the Ponzi schemes unravelled, Naveen, as the chief minister, quickly attempted to disassociate himself from all those who came under a cloud. Unlike Mamata Banerjee, his vociferous counterpart in West Bengal, who screamed and shouted, alleging a central government plot to undermine her by implicating her ministers, MPs and MLAs in similar scams, Naveen did not publicly bat for his jailed partymen. Many believed they paid the price for Naveen's time-tested credo – 'from the moment you are caught, you are on your own'. For most Odias, Naveen had already enforced in his home state the principle of '*Na khaunga, na khaney dunga* (Neither will I take bribes, nor will I allow anyone else to take them)'. This was long before Prime Minister Narendra Modi stated the same in a rousing speech. That corruption existed in Odisha on the ground, in spite of Naveen, was a different story altogether.

Aside from his anti-corruption image, burnishing Naveen's reputation had been the quiet work that had been undertaken at the grassroots level in Odisha. Panchanan Kanungo, once Naveen's finance minister, fell out of Naveen's good books a long time ago. Kanungo lost his re-election bid from his assembly constituency in Gobindpur, and Naveen, true to character, put him in cold storage. Kanungo pointed to an array of affirmative actions that the government had undertaken soon after Naveen became chief minister. Many of the measures were not big-ticket announcements, but they made huge differences across villages and panchayats. Hand receipt accounts (HRA) – unauthenticated receipts for money supposedly paid to vendors – that allowed engineering department staff to inflate expenses were done away with, tenders were made compulsory in awarding contracts and lotteries were made mandatory for allocation of houses under the Indira Awaas Yojana. 'Good image instils greater confidence, but people also want good results,' said Kanungo. 'Naveen did not disappoint.'

But a top bureaucrat who worked closely with the chief minister had another, altogether more cynical explanation for Naveen's continuing popularity. 'His biggest achievement was that he did nothing that was spectacularly wrong,' the official said. In a state where earlier chief ministers were known to lurch from one blunder to another, Naveen set a new benchmark of not making wrong decisions.'

Janardan Pati, a veteran leader of the CPM, attributed much of Naveen's success to his non-interfering and non-oppressive ways – his light touch. The veteran Marxist cited a relatively recent example to illustrate his point. Thousands of anganwadi workers converged on Bhubaneswar in the autumn of 2017 to press their demands, including a wage hike. The protesting women, noisy and itching for a showdown, blocked a city thoroughfare for more than a month. Unlike other state governments which probably would have cracked down on them, Naveen's administration looked the other way. The women were allowed to squat on the road, disrupt traffic and vent their anger until they got tired and their tempers cooled down. They dispersed and went back home several weeks after they had arrived, though the government met their demand only partially by agreeing to a marginal raise in their salary.

According to Pati, Naveen's non-confrontational approach had also bailed him out of what could have been the chief minister's 'Nandigram moment'. Nandigram, in West Bengal's Midnapore district, was the CPM-led Left Front government's Waterloo, where a farmers' protest against land acquisition for industry led to a violent crackdown and the death of fourteen people in 2007. The deaths and the brutality unleashed jointly by the police and the CPM goons outraged Bengal and the rest of the country. It eroded farmer and middle-class support for the communists, who had been ruling the state for more than three decades, and resulted in the decimation of the CPM government in elections a few years later.

Naveen, too, had come close to confronting his own Nandigram at Kalinganagar in Jajpur district in 2006. Some 30,000 acres of land had been handed over years ago to the Odisha Industrial Infrastructure Development Corporation (IIDCO) to set up the Kalinganagar Industrial Complex. The land acquired included 13,000 acres owned by tribals and government land on which locals cultivated. Nothing happened for years until IIDCO parcelled out the land to private companies, including the Tatas. But when the Tatas arrived to take possession of their land, the tribals protested, demanding higher compensation, at current market rates. They were angry that IIDCO had bought their land in 1994 at ₹37,000 an acre, but sold it to the Tatas some years later at ₹3,50,000 an acre.

Trouble erupted in 2006 and the angry tribals attacked and killed a policeman. The police retaliated, killing thirteen tribals and chopping off the slain protesters' hands. The situation was explosive and could have got infinitely worse. Besides damaging Naveen's administrative record, the deaths were ammunition for political opponents to whip up passions against him. Angry tribals blocked the highway connecting mineral-rich Daitari to the port of Paradip for a year and political rivals kept making incendiary speeches. Unlike the CPM in West Bengal, Naveen did not send in police or partymen to wrest back control and end the blockade. He didn't visit Kalinganagar even once in the immediate wake of the firing. As time went by, the Tatas struck deals with the tribals, who had many of their demands met. The courts, too, intervened a year later and ordered the removal of the blockade. The Tata steel plant came up over time and is currently running full steam, belching out smoke from its huge chimneys. A memorial to the fallen tribals, not far away from the plant, perhaps remains the only visible reminder of the strife that Kalinganagar experienced. Peace restored, Naveen went back to administering the state as if nothing had happened.

~

At no place were people happier with Naveen than in Hinjilicut, the constituency in Ganjam that unfailingly elected him to the assembly. Hinjilicut is mostly rural, spread over twenty-one panchayats comprising fifty-seven villages. Its lush fields, famous for growing vegetables, stand silent testimony to the relative prosperity of its residents, most of whom say that the region has prospered faster since Naveen took over.

Being the chief minister's constituency came with privileges. Not far away from the periphery of the crowded Hinjilicut town stands a sprawling hospital compound amid a vast expanse of agricultural fields. Sankara Nethralaya, the non-profitable charitable trust headquartered in Chennai, has set up a superspeciality eye hospital in the area, serving as a proof of the prized status that the assembly segment enjoyed.

The region provided more proof of its exalted status. Each village in the constituency had been connected with all-weather roads and enjoys piped water supply. Electricity connectivity was 100 per cent and the achievement of the target to build toilets in rural homes was near total. The same was the case with the target to build pucca houses.

Challenges remain, and the open sewage drains that meander alongside Hinjilicut town's narrow roads are one of them. Toilets are being built in very large numbers, but people's sanitation habits are proving difficult to change. It's still difficult to disembark from a car and not step on festering human excreta on the roadside. Residents prefer to venture out under the cover of darkness and defecate in the open. But amid the accumulated filth, local officials say seeds of change are being sown. 'Things are only getting better. With more awareness, people, too, will change their habits,' said a local official. For officials like him, being posted at the chief minister's constituency brought many privileges. For one, government files moved faster. Red tape normally never came in the way, and mobilizing resources for schemes and projects proved far easier.

Hinjilicut's relative prosperity reflected in Naveen's handsome victory margins time and again. In 2000, he won with a margin of 26,417 votes. In 2004, it was 24,624. By 2009, it was 61,273, which further swelled to 76,586 votes in 2014. In 2019, the margin stayed more than 60,000 with Naveen cornering 66.32 per cent of the votes that had been casted. That Naveen scraped through with only about 4,000 votes in 2024, when his rule ended, is a different story.

'My work speaks for itself,' said Naveen, while being the chief minister in a rare interview with the *India Today* magazine. To administer the state with an estimated 100 lakh households spread over 1,17,000 habitations, including 58,000 revenue villages that were spread across forests, hills and valleys, Naveen as the chief minister relied heavily on the bureaucracy – a reliance that often brought him criticism. Even ruling party members were miffed at the influence that IAS officers – in more recent times, one particular IAS officer – carried with Naveen. Ministers, too, were not happy as they survived only at the mercy of Naveen while bureaucrats seemingly carried greater influence. 'It was a government by, of and for the third floor,' recollected an aggrieved minister, referring to some influential bureaucrats who reportedly controlled everything from the chief minister's office on the third floor of the state secretariat.

However maligned or misunderstood, the bureaucrats delivered when another deadly storm, Cyclone Phailin, struck the state in October 2013 and threatened death and destruction on the same scale as the 1999 supercyclone. This cyclone, too, had winds of over 220 kilometres an hour at its peak. Nineteen of the state's thirty districts were in its path, endangering 130 lakh people. But unlike the last time when the supercyclone caught Odisha ill-prepared, leaving 10,000 people dead and the survivors drowning in distress, 'Team Naveen' was largely successful in mitigating human suffering. Days before the cyclone made its landfall, Mission Zero Casualty was launched and a concerned chief minister trooped into the office of the special relief commissioner on a Sunday to take stock. Around 10 lakh people from some of the most vulnerable locations were physically shifted to safety. As the cyclone hit, raged and passed, only 21 lives were lost.

'It was only efficiency that was at a premium under Naveen,' gushed a senior serving bureaucrat. According to him, only those who were honest, efficient and also modest found favour in Naveen's dispensation. Many bureaucrats remain effusive in their praise of the non-interfering Naveen and claim to be very proud of what has been achieved under him. The statistics they reel out justify their pride – Odisha's own tax-to-GDP ratio has increased from 3.56 per cent in 1999–2000 to 6.4 per cent in 2023–24; its own non-tax gross state domestic product (GSDP) ratio rose from 1.50 per cent in 1999–2000 to 6.3 per cent in 2023–24; its total revenue GSDP ratio increased from 5.05 per cent to 12.24 per cent over the same period. Proof of better fiscal management also lay in the state's expenditure on salaries, which came down from 160.57 per cent in 1999–2000 to about 18 per cent in 2023–24. The state's total committed expenditure – comprising salary, pension and interest payment – was also reduced from 240.15 per cent in 1999–2000 to 32 per cent in 2023–24.

Once in deficit and forced to import food from Punjab and Haryana, Odisha now is a surplus state in rice production and the third largest contributor to the country's rice granary.

The state, officials say, is in much better health today than ever in the past. The infant mortality rate has dropped by 25 points and is now on a par with the national average of 40 (that is, there are 40 deaths of children under the age of one per 1,000 live births). Maternal mortality also declined from 367 in 1998 (this refers to the number of deaths of mothers per 1,00,000 live births) to 222 in 2012–13, though the state has to do more to be on a par with the national average, which dropped from 407 to 167 during the same period. An innovative cash transfer scheme, 'Mamata', for 25 lakh pregnant and nursing mothers helped reduce infant and mother mortality rates, and the scheme was replicated by the Central government.

The list of the advances and achievements made during Naveen's tenure, officials claim, is very long.

Naveen, too, never let go of any opportunity to burnish his image – justified or not. In 2017, an opportunity presented itself when *Outlook* – the English news magazine that I came to edit as the chief editor a year later – decided to honour someone as the Best Chief Minister at its annual SpeakOut event. There was no jury or a proper selection process, and the first choice fell on Nitish Kumar. But the Bihar chief minister excused himself, saying he was too busy to attend the function to be held in Delhi. The magazine then decided on Naveen, and the Odisha chief minister readily agreed to come. The

Best Chief Minister Award, given at a glittering ceremony attended among others by former President of India, Pranab Mukherjee, did a world of good for Naveen. As always, Naveen kept quiet during the ceremony other than exchanging formal pleasantries with the other VIPs. But once the function was over and Naveen flew back to Bhubaneswar, he ensured his party made a huge song and dance over the award. Some 10,000 people greeted him upon his arrival while giant hoardings went up across the state, hailing him as the best CM. Amidst all the hype, few bothered to ask how and why he was chosen to be the best CM. But even years later, his ruling BJD made it a point to remind people that its leader was the best in the country.

There had, of course, been a number of failures too – some of them monumental. These included the botched plan to set up a giant steel plant in Paradip on Odisha's coast. Naveen had signed an agreement amid massive fanfare with the South Korean steel giant POSCO for a 12 billion tonne plant to be built at a cost of ₹52,000 crore. Billed as the single biggest foreign investment in India, the proposed steel plant was marketed as a showpiece by the Naveen government to pluck the state out of poverty and backwardness and put it on the road to prosperity. It was presented as a project that would help utilize the state's natural resources, generate employment, provide livelihoods and change the face of Odisha for the better. However, the project got nowhere. Locals resisted moves to acquire their land for the plant and a popular agitation beat back every attempt by the administration to get the project going. Finally, POSCO gave up, announcing they were not interested any more. It was a huge loss of face for Naveen and opened him up to public derision.

There had been other setbacks, too. Despite all the talk of better human development indices, the state continued to often make news for the wrong reasons. Human misery and deprivation continued to be rampant and tens of thousands were left lo live in abject penury. Dana Majhi, a poor tribal of Kalahandi district, made international headlines in 2016 when he was forced to carry the body of his dead wife for several kilometres with his daughter walking by his side and crying inconsolably. His wife had died in a hospital which had no ambulances or a hearse van, and Majhi had no money to hire a vehicle to transport the body home. Majhi's desperation highlighted the indignity, both in life and in death, that people routinely are forced to shoulder in the state. The death of nineteen children in three months in the remote Nagada cluster of villages in Jajpur district in 2017 was a human and also a public relations disaster. The government said the deaths were due to an outbreak of pneumonia and measles but opponents insisted malnutrition was the cause. It sullied Naveen's image.

The blemishes allowed critics to take potshots at him. 'The bottom line is that Odisha remained high on despair and low on hope,' contended Biswajit Mohanty, an environmental-cum-RTI activist, who was fiercely critical of Naveen.

But Naveen made up for the bad publicity by collecting goodwill with, for example, every helping of rice and *dalma* (watery lentil with vegetables) served at places such as the tin-roofed rectangular hall adjacent to the city bus stand outside the Bhubaneswar railway station. It was here the government of Naveen Patnaik fed people on a first-come, first-served basis for just ₹5 a meal. Called 'Aahar', the canteens, launched all over Odisha by Naveen, formed a part of a welfare initiative that evidently had been copied from the Amma Canteens that were run by the Tamil Nadu government of J. Jayalalithaa.

Naveen and Jayalalithaa were supposed to be friends, sharing many similarities. Both were lonely in private life and both ran their respective political parties as their fiefdom. Politicians say that when it came to inner party democracy, even the more mercurial Mamata Banerjee's Trinamool Congress fared better than Jayalalithaa's All India Anna Dravida Munnertra Kazhagam (AIADMK) or Naveen's BJD.

Naveen and Jayalalithaa, it turns out, also shared a liking for populist schemes, commonly called sops. Jayalalithaa showered sops and more sops on her people during her lifetime. The Amma Canteens were her most successful signature sop and Naveen had them replicated in Odisha.

Strategically located outside bus stations, railway stations and state hospitals, the Aahar canteens target the poor. There are 167 of them in total – including 58 of them located near hospitals – being run across the state's thirty districts, with money coming from state-run corporations such as the Odisha Mining Corporation (OMC). Local-level organizations such as rice miller associations also contribute. The food served was hot and hygienic, and Naveen, whose giant posters covered the canteen walls end to end, earned the good wishes of the people who ate at the outlets every day. The inside walls of the canteen outside the Bhubaneswar railway station had no less than fourteen Naveen posters, impressing even visually impaired citizens like Shib Charan Raut from Jagatsinghpur. 'Naveen Babu is very kind. I see a better future for people,' Raut said, while savouring the rice and dalma with two companions who, like him, could not see Naveen's face smiling at them from the posters.

Many others who came to eat at the Aahar canteens shared similar views. Run initially at an annual expenditure of ₹32 crores, the food served at the subsidized canteens had become so popular that even the banquet manager of a swanky hotel not far from the Aahar canteen outside the Bhubaneswar railway station visited the canteen stealthily a couple of times a week to have a cheap but nutritious meal. Given the noble intention behind the canteens, no political party came out publicly to criticize the initiative. But opposition leaders did maintain that, just like Jayalalithaa, Naveen had mastered the art of squandering money on subsidies and sops. 'The sops made people happy. Though the state may not have progressed, people felt satisfied,' said Rita Ray, a retired professor of sociology at Utkal University. Sanjaya Kumar Jena, the chief editor of Argus TV channel, agreed that the sops and subsidies served Naveen well. 'His sops scratched the surface and did not address the real issues, but they helped in giving people a false high and kept them happy,' he said.

The poor, the infirm, the disabled, the retired, the tribals, old women, young women, pregnant mothers, lactating mothers – name any section of people and Naveen, in all likelihood, had a sop or two for them. His government ran dozens of welfare schemes such as the Gopabandhu Grameen Yojana (for rural development), Biju Pucca Ghar Yojana (for building brick houses), Madhu Babu Pension Yojana (for providing pension to the poor and infirm), Mukhya Mantri Sadak Yojana (for the development of roads), Biju Atma Nijukti Yojana (for self-employment) and Biju Setu Yojana (for building bridges). The schemes were meant to expedite development and provide relief in certain key areas. In addition to this, Naveen had been intervening and reaching out to his people with bespoke innovative measures. It started in 2004 when he announced a compensation of ₹25,000 for any tribal falling ill from contaminated food. If any tribal woman was sexually exploited, she would get a compensation of ₹50,000. More interestingly, if a wage earner in a tribal family was to be imprisoned in a case for more than ten years, his family would be given a grant of ₹50,000 by the government.

In 2005, the Odisha government announced free uniforms and cycles to about 14 lakh students in 142 educationally backward blocks of the state, besides an insurance cover of ₹25,000 each for 68 lakh school children in the state. The Madhu Babu Pension Yojana, started in 2008, promised a monthly payout to 43 lakh people at a cost of ₹700 crore annually. Widows of any age, leprosy patients, those with mental health issues or with cerebral palsy were among those entitled for assistance under the scheme named after Madhusudan Das, the man who led the movement for the creation of a separate Odisha state.

From time to time, Naveen's government came up with new schemes covering newer sections of the community. It gave free cycles to 1.7 lakh girl students studying in class 10 in government and government-aided schools and introduced assistance of ₹5,000 to pregnant and lactating women. Free cycles to girls were followed by free cycles to 1.6 lakh students in the below poverty line (BPL) category. In 2012, the government gave ₹200 each to 37 lakh senior citizens, widows and physically challenged persons to buy blankets. Free umbrellas were distributed to 33 lakh widows, destitutes and the differently abled. In a God-fearing state where Lord Jagannath rules the hearts and minds, even servitors of the Puri temple were not forgotten. The government promised free houses to those among them without home or land, free education and scholarships ranging from ₹100 to ₹500 to their children studying in classes 1 to 10 and ₹25,000 for those pursuing technical education, besides an insurance cover of ₹2 lakh for their families.

The measures, big and small, went a long way in garnering goodwill for Naveen as the chief minister. But the biggest game changer of all was in 2008 when Naveen announced 25 kilos of rice at only ₹2 a kilo for the 55 lakh BPL families in the state. Rice at this rate was also made available to all families, irrespective of their income, in the historically poorer districts of undivided Kalahandi, Balangir and Koraput. The rice scheme established the chief minister's welfare credentials and helped him win votes in the assembly elections in 2009. Among everything else that he did to stay on the right side of popular sentiments, including replacing about 30 per cent of sitting MLAs with fresh faces as party candidates, the rice scheme brought him the biggest and best dividend. Subsequently he bettered the rice scheme in 2013, providing rice at only ₹1 to 48 lakh BPL families in the state. Needless to say, the beneficiaries of the scheme were seen as the strongest section of Naveen's support base, right until the central government made the rice totally free. Naveen could no more take credit, and he paid an electoral price in 2024.

The rice scheme caused immense heartburn among Naveen's opponents and sparked a political slugfest with the BJP. Eyeing to unseat Naveen in 2019 and seize political power in the state, BJP Central ministers accused Naveen of appropriating credit for schemes that are bankrolled by the Central government. 'It is not Naveen rice, but Modi rice,' insisted the then Union Minister Prakash Javadekar during a visit to Odisha for the purpose of strengthening the party's organization and boosting the morale of its workers.

According to BJP leaders, the rice that Naveen provided to the people for ₹1 actually cost ₹32 a kilogram. Of this, the central government paid ₹29 a kilo, the state government paid ₹2 and the consumer paid ₹1. The commonest grouse consequently among BJP leaders in the state was that Naveen ran away for much of his tenure with all the credit though he did not deserve it.

But politics is all about perceptions, and Naveen won on that score squarely over the years. Rivals accused the ruling BJD of adopting practices, often unfair, to appropriate publicity and the resultant goodwill. They alleged that block-level government officials told beneficiaries of houses under Indira Awas Yojana to put up plaques proclaiming 'Biju Patnaik Awaas' though the subsidy for the scheme was borne by the central government. With the BJD being in power for 24 years, local officials allegedly worked as extensions of the ruling party and had become grossly partisan. Outlets that distributed subsidized rice at ₹1 carried pictures of a smiling, 'benevolent' Naveen. At some places, the opposition alleged, recipients were told that Naveen was the benefactor.

With a member-strength of one crore, the ruling BJD managed to dictate and dominate the messages across the state. It ceaselessly amplified Naveen's pro-poor work. The party machinery, including its field organizations which covered youth, women, OBCs and other targeted groups, helped continuously to drive home the point that there was no one better than Naveen in the state. Popular acceptance of the TINA (there is no alternative) theory also worked to the ruling party's advantage for a very long period.

Given the party's robust organization, it was no surprise that the residents of Juang Sahi, a tribal village of thirty-seven households in the remote Telkoi block in Keonjhar district, were convinced that Naveen was their sole saviour. 'It is Naveen Babu who gave us the rice,' insisted Damodar Juang, slightly high on his evening *handia*, the locally manufactured brew. Others not so intoxicated agreed readily, nodding in approval at Naveen's name. They recognized only Naveen among all the other Odisha politicians, though they conceded having heard the name of Prime Minister Narendra Modi as well.

The BJP – as Odisha's principal opposition party since it dislodged the Congress from that position – tried hard to counter what it called the 'misinformation' and chose to highlight the contributions of Modi. It attempted to counter the BJD's choreographed narrative of Naveen being an extremely caring ruler, who personally gave people everything from pensions to rice and blankets, cycles and shoes. The party took pains to explain to people that the majority of

Naveen's schemes were actually the generosity of Prime Minister Modi. The biggest slugfest was over taking credit for the subsidized rice. The rice that was given was cheap, but the political dividend that the scheme fetched was huge and the BJP spared no effort to raise awareness among common people that it was a central government scheme. And when the rice became totally free, it bolstered BJP's prospects.

The challenges mounted by the BJP in 2019 and then again in 2024 were something of a new experience for Naveen. The opposition in the state had been in disarray ever since he first became chief minister in 2000. 'Naveen was fortunate since he was never really seriously challenged in the first few terms. He kept getting walkovers after walkovers,' said Rabi Das, the Bhubaneswar-based political commentator. The Congress lacked a leader or a talking point and never managed to mount a serious challenge to the BJD. In early 2004, the Congress attempted to resurrect its fortunes by bringing back J.B. Patnaik as the state party president. Though unpopular, Patnaik was an organizational man and the party hoped he would be in a position to pull off a miracle in time for the next assembly election in 2005. Naveen, however, pulled the rug from under their feet by ordering snap polls. J.B. Patnaik was made the Pradesh Congress Committee (PCC) chief on 14 January 2004 and

Naveen ordered the dissolution of the state assembly and early elections on 29 January 2024.

The BJP also found the going tough. It was a Naveen ally until 2009. When it fell out with him, the saffron party had neither a leader nor the organizational might to take on the BJD. It was only after it attained power in Delhi in 2014 that it began to seriously flex its muscles, hoping to ride on Prime Minister Modi's charm to counter Naveen's charisma.

But checkmating Naveen was never easy. Opposition leaders, big and small, over the years, hurled every possible accusation at him without making any impact. Snide remarks and comments were passed, and even Naveen's sexuality had been questioned, even though it had nothing to do with politics. But Naveen survived the concerted attacks, both on his person and on the party. 'The combined credibility of all opposition leaders put together was not able to match the credibility that Naveen came to enjoy as an individual,' said Rita Ray, the sociology professor at Utkal University.

Members of one group, in particular, vouched vociferously for Naveen's integrity. They were an overwhelming majority of Odisha's 200 lakh women who formed the bedrock of his political support. Though Naveen was a bachelor, his emotional bonding with the state's womenfolk was remarkable. Soon after he became chief minister, he set his eyes on setting up self-help groups (SHGs) for women across Odisha's rural landscape. Branded 'Mission Shakti', the initiative caught on and became a movement. Odisha now has about 6 lakh SHGs. That made for about 60 lakh women who presumably were benefited from easy bank loans and set up their own enterprises. They were all Naveen's committed voters.

Those committed voters included women like Anupama Behera of Gopinathpur in Ganjam district and her neighbours, Sajani Behera and Geeta Behera. Their lives did not count for much earlier. But once SHGs began to be formed, they, too, floated their own and were helped to gain access to easy loans. It allowed the women to make packaged *chatua* (a ready-to-eat fortified powder of wheat, dal, cashew etc.) that the district administration bought for distribution among mothers to feed their infants. The women also collected payments for electricity bills in their neighbourhood for a fee of ₹5 for every bill collected. Work was hard, but also remunerative. Each member of the group made an average of ₹5,000 a month. 'Our value at home went up. We were taken more seriously,' said Sajani Behera. Anupama, who could afford to pay the fees of her engineering-student son, agreed. 'I became the man at home,' she said grinning proudly. Village after village in Odisha had similar such tales of empowerment to tell. Helped with loans at nominal interest rates, women got together to weave and realize their dreams. From fishing and agriculture and horticulture to making bangles and bindis, the women's collectives were into myriad activities, but all with the common objective of empowering women. The National Family Health Survey (NHFS) bore out some of the positive changes that the SHGs ushered in. Compared to the NFHS survey of 2015–16 when only 81.8 per cent of women were found to be participating in household decision-making, 90.2 per cent of women were found to be taking part in decisions taken at their respective homes in the 2019–21 NFHS survey. More women got elected to Panchayati raj institutions from gram panchayats to zilla parishads as Naveen extended his rule term after term.

Reaping the benefits, tens of thousands of Odisha women readily gave Naveen the credit for changing their lives. 'But for him, this would not have been possible,' said Anupama Behera. 'The SHGs were Naveen's biggest political capital,' admitted Panchanan Kanungo, the former finance minister. Besides the SHGs, the women were also appreciative of Naveen's quiet ways. 'Naveen's silence, after all, was his eloquence,' explained Kishor Kumar Basa, a professor in Utkal University later appointed as chairman of National Museum Authority. 'Naveen gave the women of the state a sense of security that no other chief minister had given,' said Pratap Keshari Deb, a senior BJD leader.

With women firmly behind him, winning elections were fairly easy for Naveen. In 2000, only 54 per cent of the eligible women voters came out to vote. But in 2014, the elections in which Naveen withstood and worsted the Modi wave, the turnout of women was as high as 74 per cent. With women coming out in large numbers, it wasn't difficult to guess who would win. Naveen, too, drove home the point by relentlessly publicizing the role of SHGs in uplifting lives. In 2019, he actually nominated an SHG member, Pramila Bisoyi, as the party candidate for the Lok Sabha elections from Aska (which he once represented). Once elected, the septuagenarian Bisoyi rarely spoke in parliament. But Naveen's act of fielding a SHG member as a candidate spoke loudly, ingratiating him with the women further.

Never shy of entertaining people with the most quotable quotes, irrespective of how tough it has been for his own Congress party, veteran politician Suresh Kumar Routray summed it up inimitably: *'Odishara stree mane Naveenanka sathire preeti karicchanti* (Odisha's women are in love with Naveen)', Routray said hours after Naveen won in 2014. The love for

Naveen brought in the desired results regularly. In 2019, when the BJP launched a full frontal attack against the BJD, its then state president Kanak Vardhan Singh Deo had pompously predicted an impending tsunami. Of course, a tsunami struck, but it largely swept away the BJP in the elections for the state assembly. Naveen's party won 112 of the total 147 seats while the BJP remained a distant second, winning just 23 seats. The groundswell of love that existed for Naveen had successfully staved off another storm. And Naveen continued to be in the chief minister's chair – until the next general elections came knocking in 2024.

5

2024: The Pandian Puzzle

The year 2024 brought several surprises to Odisha, the foremost being the near-total dominance of V. Karthikeyan Pandian in the social and political discourse in the state. Pandian, a middle-level IAS officer hailing from Tamil Nadu, got his parent cadre of Punjab changed to Odisha on getting married to an Odisha-cadre colleague from the 2000 batch of IAS officers. Fifty-year-old Pandian turned out to be a giant phenomenon grossly disproportionate to his diminutive size.

Not more than five-feet-five-inches in height, the slim Pandian – in his trademark outfit of tight trousers, a full-sleeves shirt that he never tucked and a pair of casual chappals – occupied the centerstage like no one else (including his boss Naveen Patnaik), and stoked a political storm that raged and refused to subside until the 2024 general elections and the unseating of the ruling BJD.

Most Odias were amazed at the influence that the IAS officer – engaged earlier as the private secretary to chief minister Naveen – wielded. Though his profile had been growing since long, many were aghast at the prominence that Pandian finally came to occupy. In October 2023, Pandian quit the IAS and a month later, took the plunge into politics by joining his boss's BJD. He touched Naveen's feet amid a publicity blitz and joined the ruling party. Technically, he remained only an 'ordinary' worker of the party. He held no party post, though a visibly pleased Naveen instantly gave him a plum government position – making him chairman of his government's 5T initiative with focus on transparency, technology, teamwork, time and transformation, with a cabinet minister's rank.

Pandian's public profile skyrocketed after he joined politics. He hogged all the headlines, sidelining other prominent BJD ministers and leaders. Even an ageing Naveen – more reclusive than ever before – was eclipsed, as senior partymen competed with one another to make a beeline for Pandian and pay obeisance to him. At party rallies in the run-up to the polls, Pandian strode up to elabourate stages to address crowds alone, while ministers and MLAs sat below. The more exuberant amongst them bowed before Pandian publicly. In Balasore in coastal Odisha, a senior minister from an erstwhile royal family as well as the BJD organization secretary got down from their respective cars to give Pandian's convoy smooth passage in an unabashed show of sycophancy.

The problem though was the poor optics that the display of public grovelling generated. More than awe – which perhaps was the original intent – Pandian succeeded in putting off a very large section of the public. Soon, he became a lightening rod and a deeply polarizing figure.

Most horrified by Pandian's preeminence was one retired IAS officer – the man singularly responsible for plucking Pandian out of bureaucratic anonymity and putting him on the path to power, fame and infamy. But for this retired officer – once known for his proximity to Naveen – Pandian would possibly have ended up as just another one of Odisha's 200-odd IAS men and women who work behind their desks through their professional careers, rising through the ranks gradually to occupy more important positions, before finally retiring and slipping back into oblivion.

Pandian's initial career trajectory seemed to move no differently. After graduating from the Lal Bahadur Shastri National Academy of Administration and getting his cadre changed to Odisha after marrying Sujata Rout, an Odia IAS officer with roots in the state's Kendrapara district, Pandian made his administrative debut as sub-collector of the dusty

Dharamgarh town in Kalahandi district in 2002. Some two years later, he was appointed the additional district magistrate of the Rourkela Development Agency that he reportedly turned around financially during his short stint. He then became the collector of Mayurbhanj, the district that India's current president Droupadi Murmu hails from. In 2007, Pandian was transferred and made collector of Ganjam, the district for which Naveen as the chief minister held a special interest. After all, his assembly constituency – Hinjilicut – fell within Ganjam.

Though lowkey in those days, Pandian proved himself to be an able officer. Hardworking and disciplined, with a habit of starting his day at 4 a.m., Pandian had a modest background: he had stayed at a government-run sports hostel when he was younger and was a middle-distance runner. He worked tirelessly and helped in streamlining the disbursement of certificates and benefits to persons with disabilities in Mayurbhanj.

His work got noticed and he caught the attention of the earlier mentioned IAS officer, who is now retired. Always on the lookout for talent and to draft efficient officers in the chief minister's office, the bureaucrat had his eyes on three officers – Ashok Dalwai, G. Mathi Vathanan and Pandian – in that order. The retired officer wished to bring in Dalwai in a senior post to the chief minister's office (CMO), possibly as principal secretary, but Dalwai was not interested. When the opportunity arose to appoint a new official to the relatively junior position of private secretary to the chief minister, Mathi Vathanan got the call. But that turned out to be a short-term experiment. Naveen could be snappy – particularly in the mornings when he arrived at work after having met senior party leaders at home. These party leaders invariably had a never-ending list of demands and Naveen normally started his day at the CMO in a foul mood. Unable to cope, Mathi Vathanan opted out in about a year's time.

The search for a new private secretary to replace Mathi Vathanan turned out to be a turning point. Next in the order of choice for the senior bureaucrat was Pandian and he got posted to the CM's office in 2011. Once in the CMO, both luck and hard labour helped Pandian cement his place in double-quick time.

Always diligent, the new secretary made a good impression to begin with. It improved infinitely some months later when Pyari Mohan Mohapatra – the ex-bureaucrat-advisor of Naveen's – initiated what is generally considered to have been a coup attempt in 2012. Naveen was abroad and needed help to launch a counter-offensive. This meant calling up legislators back home and sweet-talking them into not deserting the BJD ship. Given his laidback nature, Naveen needed someone to work the phone, make calls and rally support of his MLAs, and Pandian gladly stepped in for this task. Grabbing the unexpected opportunity with both hands, he reached out to MLAs on behalf of the beleaguered chief minister, and helped Naveen navigate the crisis. Pandian's stock rose immeasurably.

Pandian began to pack quite a powerful punch despite being just a private secretary. The importance of seniors in the CMO began to dwindle as Pandian gradually became the eyes and ears of Naveen. High-ranking bureaucrats outside the CMO felt the change in power dynamics too. A mild-mannered state chief secretary sought deputation to the central government in Delhi, months before his tenure was to end. He found it unbearable and beneath his dignity to continue. Thereafter followed a chain of chief secretaries – one less powerful and seemingly more accommodating of Pandian than the last. Chief secretaries came and went, while Pandian consolidated. One particular chief secretary was benched three months prior to his retirement, to be replaced by someone more submissive.

The CMO, too, underwent a change. A coterie – comprising officials handpicked by Pandian – was formed and they called the shots. Adding teeth to this group was an IPS officer who was brought in. It was unusual for the CMO to have a police official, and Naveen did not have one during his first fifteen years as CM. Even his father Biju Patnaik did not have one. The only other chief minister to have had an IPS official in his office was J.B. Patnaik in the 1990s, and that was a period Odisha had little to be proud of.

From being known to be benign, soft and friendly in the earlier years, the government headed by Naveen increasingly showed signs of heavy-handedness, if not vindictiveness. In 2018, Baijayant 'Jay' Panda – once a Naveen confidant and now a freshly elected BJP member of parliament – faced the brunt of it.

Soft-spoken, suave and well-networked, Panda was the face of the BJD in Delhi. Given his friendship with Naveen, he was made a Rajya Sabha MP in 2000. He continued to be a member of the Upper House till 2009, when he contested the Lok Sabha elections from Kendrapara and won. He was re-elected in 2014.

So far so good, and Panda served Naveen's needs well for years. Besides occasionally giving the chief minister company in the evenings, Panda was rich and influential. His industrialist family had deep pockets and his wife ran OTV, Odisha's most popular television channel with an unmatched reach. But insiders say that relations between Panda and Naveen began to sour since the media started speculating about Naveen's health around 2015–2016, and there was talk that the chief minister would shortly visit London for a liver transplant.

Given his history of sidelining potential rivals, it was natural that Naveen wouldn't trust Panda completely. The MP was too rich and well-connected for the chief minister's comfort. That his wife owned a popular television channel, which could be used to push his political agenda, was also perhaps not lost on Naveen. Also, Panda's comparison to Biju Patnaik by some of Naveen's courtiers had put Naveen off. Like Biju Babu, Panda was tall, a trained pilot and had a Punjabi wife. Biju Babu's wife Gyan was a Punjabi as well. But whatever be the real reasons, the parting between Panda and Naveen was abrupt and acrimonious. The invitations for Panda to visit Naveen Niwas dried up and the MP was stripped of his position as the BJD parliamentary party spokesman. As he became persona non grata within the party, he found the going tough. Ruling partymen began opposing his visits to his constituency and he was also physically attacked.

Panda hit back, accusing Naveen and his party of forsaking its original path and principles. One thing led to another, and the relationship soured beyond repair. In January 2018, Panda publicly targeted Pandian. Though he did not take any names, he accused a certain non-Odia IAS officer in the chief minister's office of protecting antisocial elements. He also issued a press statement alleging that this officer was interfering in party affairs and unconstitutionally indulging in politics.

Panda was suspended from the party and accused of having a conflict of interest. The BJD said that Panda drew Rs 1.45 crores as salary and allowances from his family-owned company. Cut to size, Panda continued his tirade against Naveen for some time. He finally quit the party in May 2018, shortly after his industrialist father Bansidhar Panda died.

The elder Panda had been Odisha's pioneering industrialist, besides being a close friend of Biju Patnaik's. The two families were close and Panda called Biju Babu 'Biju uncle'. As the senior Panda's body lay for people to pay their respects – first at his home in Bomikhal, Bhubaneswar, and then at his village home of Madhuban, Báranga – hundreds streamed in, but not a single prominent BJD leader came. A grieving and heartbroken Panda resigned from the BJD soon after. 'That the BJD does not want me anymore, and in fact wants me out, is now irrefutably clear,' he wrote in his emotional resignation letter.

Panda's resignation made national news. He quit as a Lok Sabha MP some days later. Stung by the criticism on social media of what many felt was sheer 'meanness' of the BJD top brass in the wake of senior Panda's death, some party leaders did show up for the eleventh-day rituals. They included then state minister Prafulla Samal, MP Prasanna Patsani and MLA Debasis Nayak. The BJD men in attendance were, however, far outnumbered by leaders from other political parties such as the BJP's Dharmendra Pradhan, Giridhar Gamang and the state Congress president Niranjan Patnaik.

Things went from bad to worse thereafter. Panda was hosting two visiting acquaintances from Delhi a few months later and decided to fly them on his private helicopter over the famous Sun temple in Konark and the pristine Chilika lake, famous for its dancing dolphins. One of the two guests made a crass joke about Odisha and put it out on social media, inviting instant opprobrium. Local sentiments were hurt; the guest was jailed for some weeks. Panda, too, found himself in hot water. He was accused by the state government of violating an imaginary no-fly zone over Chilika and had cases registered against him. Worse still, his helicopter hangar, which housed his private choppers in a corner of Bhubaneswar airport, was seized. Naveen's government had his entire fleet grounded. Deprived of mobility, Panda's plans for touring across the state to drum up popular support for himself flew out of the window.

That the cases registered against him finally came to nought did not deter Naveen's government. The Director General of Civil Aviation (DGCA) gave Panda a clean chit, certifying that he had not violated any rules. But the Odisha government was not done with him, and in 2020, his wife's OTV channel found itself in the crosshairs of an administration seemingly seeking to teach the Pandas a lesson.

The channel, despite its wide reach, faced an official boycott from the ruling BJD. None of its leaders or spokespersons would come to the channel to participate in discussions or debates. The channel was also invariably not invited to official functions. The Covid crisis brought in further trouble.

All hell broke loose in June 2020 after OTV aired a conversation between two Covid patients discussing alleged mismanagement and corruption during the pandemic in state hospitals. In August, the channel reported that Naveen had falsely claimed to have done an aerial survey of some flood-affected districts. OTV was only reporting the claims of some information rights activists who produced necessary documents from the Bhubaneswar airport authority to show that only one helicopter had taken off from the airport the day Naveen was said to have conducted the aerial survey and was airborne for just 19 minutes – including the time required for taking off and landing.

It was impossible for Naveen to have reached any of the flood-affected districts in such a short time, the activists claimed.

Shortly thereafter, officials from the Bhubaneswar Municipal Corporation (BMC) lodged police complaints against the channel, invoking sections under the Indian Penal Code and the Epidemic Diseases Act. The accusation was that the channel had misreported and misrepresented facts. The police swung into action and senior OTV staff – the chief editor, HR head, input and output editors – were repeatedly summoned to police stations. Police teams even reached the native village of Chief Editor Radhamadhav Mishra and questioned his relatives. More trouble followed with several private hospitals such as the Hi-Tech Hospital and the Sum Hospital also registering criminal complaints against OTV. By then, it was virtually raining complaints. A BJD MP, Anubhav Mohanty, initiated a defamation suit against OTV for allegedly defaming him in one of their reports. The head of the investigative team of the channel was picked up and brought to a police station in connection with a complaint of a woman BJD MP regarding an objectionable video. His relatives – some engaged in small businesses – were allegedly pressured and the investigative team head resigned from OTV. OTV also had cases registered against it for allegedly encroaching on government land. Then, a former employee alleged her minor daughter had been raped by certain staffers of the channel. The state Women's Commission stepped in and repeatedly called in Panda's wife, Jagi Mangat, for questioning while the staffers were arrested. Four of them spent years in jail.

In total, 16 cases and complaints were filed against the channel in August and October 2020. Under unrelenting pressure, it is generally believed that OTV somewhat capitulated. Panda's family had other businesses to protect and OTV's coverage became somewhat subdued. It remained a critic of the state government, but the sting was missing in the stories that it aired. The police, too, stopped visiting its premises. But there was no letup in the ham-handed manner the state government sought to tame anyone and everyone. Instinctively shy and withdrawn, Naveen was never media-friendly. In his entire tenure of 24 years, he held only one press conference, that too in 2000, months after he had first assumed power. The distrust for the press got more pronounced post-2019, when Naveen got re-elected for the fifth time and Pandian came to control all levers of power in the state more publicly.

The national media, mostly headquartered in Delhi, was courted and lavished with advertisements and sponsorships. But back home in Odisha, it was a different story. A mixture of carrot and stick succeeded in securing meek compliance. With almost all mainstream newspapers and TV channels owned and run either by politicians or businessmen with political interests, it was not uncommon to find several Odia dailies carrying the same story praising Naveen with the same photograph and same headline prominently displayed on their front pages. The local press was made totally subservient but for a few rare exceptions. The government got bolder, ultimately banning the entry of journalists into the state secretariat under the pretext of Covid. The ban stayed in place right until Naveen and his BJD were defeated in 2024 – long after the pandemic had passed.

In the intervening years, BJD leaders, big and small, found Naveen increasingly inaccessible. People close to him, former MLA and minister Pradeep Panigrahi included, fell out of favour. Panigrahi – once Naveen's man Friday and caretaker of his Hinjilitcut assembly constituency – became a pariah after reportedly having a run-in with Pandian. He had corruption cases registered against him and his bank accounts were seized. He spent months in jail and helplessly saw the best-laid plans for his daughter's wedding go for a six.

Others close to Naveen found the going tough as well. They could no longer meet Naveen at Naveen

Niwas, and the only way they could meet him was to go through his secretary Pandian. And on the rare occasions they could meet, they had little opportunity to have an open chat. Many detested Pandian's growing interference and influence, and wanted to complain about him. But Pandian made it a point to be present at every meeting, and the leaders had to keep their mouth shut. Consequently, Naveen was deprived of honest feedback.

The situation got worse post Covid. Naveen had stopped working out of the CMO on the third floor of the state secretariat since he was re-elected the fifth time in 2019. Given his health and age, he preferred to operate out of his private residence. And when Covid struck, work from home became the rule, with Naveen visiting the secretariat only on rare occasions and for ceremonial purposes such as receiving a visiting dignitary. The more withdrawn Naveen became, the more powerful Pandian and his coterie grew.

Matters came to a head during the latter half of 2023, with a seemingly power-drunk Pandian stepping on the gas. Naveen's secretary had by then taken to the skies, hopping around in a helicopter to visit all 147 assembly constituencies of the state with the stated purpose of collecting public grievances on behalf of the chief minister. At some places, he took to a helicopter to travel very short distances, such as in Malkangiri, where he flew to a rally site just four kilometers away from the Malkangiri airport. The visits were grand affairs. Senior district officials, including the collector and the superintendent of police, waited to greet Pandian as and when he hit the ground, and accompany him in elaborate convoys to the site of glitzy rallies. Thousands of people – predominantly women from self-help groups – attended, and Pandian addressed them alone from the giant stages. He also took pains to take selfies with the women, just as public political figures such as Prime Minister Modi or Rahul Gandhi did.

The spectacle outraged citizens and politicians alike and Pandian's larger-than-life public profile became the subject of a heated debate in the Odisha assembly. But Naveen batted for his trusted lieutenant, insisting that he had directed him to reach out to people to listen to their grievances. The chief minister also explained that around Rs 9 crores had been spent on the helicopter rides in the past six months for Pandian to collect some 57,000 grievances.

The explanation, however, did not cut much ice. For one, Naveen did not elaborate on why it was Pandian alone who went across the state when the chief minister's office had 14 other officials, including some other IAS men and women. Did the CMO mean only Pandian?, some wondered.

Soumya Ranjan Patnaik, the influential son-in-law of former chief minister J.B. Patnaik and the owner-editor of the largest Odia daily *Sambad*, couldn't take it any longer. Also a politician – a former Congress MP who switched sides to the BJP for some time before joining the BJD to become an MLA – he wrote a front-page editorial on his 70th birthday (in August 2023), wondering who was bigger: the minister or the secretary. He followed up with three more editorials in quick succession, naming Pandian, and shining a light on the state's new phenomenon of helpless politicians and powerful bureaucrats.

Almost immediately, Soumya was forced to bear the brunt of an enraged administration. The Economic Offences Wing of the Odisha police swung into action and registered a spate of criminal cases against the *Sambad* group for alleged fraud in procuring bank loans in the name of its employees. The complainants were mostly ex-*Sambad* staffers who now worked for a rival newspaper with known links to the BJD. The loans in question dated back some fifteen years and had been repaid. Yet, the police kept visiting and *Sambad* found itself under siege. Meanwhile, Soumya was stripped of the party vice-presidentship and subsequently sacked. Simultaneously, the state government discontinued giving advertisements to the paper. Local advertisements, too, mysteriously dried up. Then, it all changed as abruptly as it had started. On 1 October, Soumya stepped down as the editor of *Sambad* and gave up all his shares in the group. His relatives took charge, and the police – just as in the case of OTV earlier – coincidentally stopped coming. The advertisers, too, returned soon after.

Though the loudest critic of Pandian's helicopter tours was silenced, the questions over the airborne visits never did really go away. Many felt that the visits were a prelude to Pandian's political launch – albeit a very costly one. They were proven right, with Pandian quitting the IAS and officially joining the BJD a few months later.

But more alleged improprieties have come to light since then. As it turns out now, the Odisha government did pay for Pandian's helicopter rides to the districts. But who paid for the hundreds of crores spent on his rallies in all 147 assembly constituencies? Government records now suggest that the state had made no budgetary allocations for them and the state did not pay for them. Where did the money come from then? Could it be that outsiders – be it contractors or corporate houses – footed the bills?

But at that point of time, Pandian's writ ran large and no one dared to challenge him. His profile grew larger and his influence bigger. Naveen by then was mostly homebound, and the reins of power slipped more and more into the hands of Pandian. The chief minister occasionally intervened. The RDC (Revenue Development Commissioner) is next only to the state chief secretary in the administrative hierarchy, and the seniormost of IAS official to fill up the post was not to Naveen's liking. He got his staff to draw up a list of other senior officials qualified to step into that position. A list of nine was drawn up and Naveen finally ticked the name of the eighth – Pradeep Jena – who rose to become the chief secretary in February 2023.

That Pandian generally enjoyed a free pass was obvious to everyone. His handpicked officials called the shots even after Pandian had joined politics. Those not in his team mattered little, and the seniormost officials in the administration silently watched their authority slipping away. Since the beginning of 2023, many of them even stopped visiting the districts, apprehending that district collectors and SPs would not show them even the customary courtesy of receiving them. Power in the state flowed from a shadowy source, and senior officials outside Pandian's charmed circle became emasculated. So much so that one chief secretary – who happened to be the last during Naveen's tenure – disagreed with many decisions taken in by the government and sent no less than 26 dissenting notes between January and

May 2024. On each occasion, someone else within the system overruled the chief secretary.

The new system did not spare even the Jagannath temple in Puri. To redevelop the precincts of the temple, where the state's presiding deity resided along with his siblings, had long been a goal of Naveen's government, and the much-publicized Shree Jagannath Parikrama Prakalpa (SPP), a wide passage around the temple walls worth Rs 800 crores, was finally unveiled amid much fanfare months before the 2024 elections. It was largely viewed as the BJD's attempt to consolidate Hindu votes in a God-fearing state.

But the day the results came out and the BJD was trounced, the lights that cast a magical spell on the majestic temple from outside suddenly went dark. Someone had turned them off and taken them away. Senior officials in the state secretariat panicked. Anything to do with the Puri temple held tremendous sentimental value for the people of Odisha, and some on social media had begun to speculate that the sudden enveloping darkness was a sign of the Lord not being happy with the election outcome. Naveen by now was just an outgoing chief minister, and his aide Pandian merely a spent force who was past his sell-by date.

The officials spent the next day or so frantically making calls. The first calls went out to the Puri temple administration authority, but they claimed ignorance. They insisted that they did not know who put up the lights in the first place as it had no official sanction and no budgetary approval. The next to be called up was the Puri district collector. But he, too, did not know. The last and final call went to managers at the Odisha Bridge and Construction Corporation Limited – a government undertaking often tasked with executing government projects. Even they did not know.

It later turned out that the outside lighting at the Puri temple was in fact unauthorized. Someone influential had called up a private contractor to put up the lighting. For months after the Parikrama Prakalpa was inaugurated, the lighting dazzled, with even the electricity service provider supplying power to the unauthorized arrangement. Everyone was glad, including the contractor who got paid from some unaccounted fund. But once the 2024 election results were out and the BJD lost, the contractor realized that getting paid in the future for his 'unapproved' work was doubtful. He dismantled the lighting and left within hours. Mortified to learn the details, the officials at the secretariat then had a locally arranged contractor put up the lights again. This time, the work was authorized.

The Puri temple episode best illustrated how unaccountable the administration had grown in Odisha overtime. The rulebook was often ignored to serve short-term goals and realise the personal interests of a few. Pandian, for one, was heavily invested in the Puri Parikrama project. He always projected himself as a devout Jagannath follower, and never tired of showcasing to visitors the initiative to improve the congested and cluttered surroundings of the temple. He clearly hoped that the blessings of Lord Jagannath and the goodwill that the Puri project could generate would help accelerate his climb to the top as a politician.

But why Naveen – generally suspicious by nature and not given to trusting anyone – chose to blindly back Pandian remains a mystery. One obvious reason could be that a bachelor Naveen, living alone in Bhubaneswar, needed someone to be dependent upon in his advanced years. While it was Pyari Mohapatra who did most of his work during his earlier years in power, Pandian stepped in during the later years. Naveen, it is said, was content being in the position of power while Pandian did all the hard work. Irrespective of the reason, Naveen banked unsuspectingly on Pandian, and senior officials, while walking up the stairs alongside the ageing chief minister, heard him mutter 'KP Boy, KP Boy' on several occasions – just as we exclaim 'Oh God!' when exasperated.

Naveen's near-total dependence on Pandian went against conventional wisdom and at least some ruling party politicians felt it was political suicide. Even the opposition BJP sensed an opportunity. Talk in roadside tea stalls, *dhaba*s and drawing rooms across the state suggested that the public wasn't too happy. They had little to say as long as Pandian stayed behind his bureaucratic cloak and pulled strings behind the scenes. But now that he had taken the political plunge and his ambition was out in the open, the rumblings began. Striking a discordant note were Pandian's Tamil origin and his heavily Tamil-accented Odia. Many were left wondering how he had come to be so important. Neither the people nor BJD partymen had elected him as the second-most important leader of ruling party after Naveen. The biggest puzzle over Pandian, therefore, was: why?

Ruling partymen had no explanations to offer. Most stayed quiet and sulked silently. Gita Mehta – Naveen's elder sister – reportedly raised the issue of Pandian. During her last days, before she passed away in Delhi in September 2023, she was reported to have voiced her concern in a feeble voice: 'I hope he is not misleading him,' she apparently confided in someone who went to visit her in the hospital.

But Naveen remained undeterred, perhaps under the misguided impression that the people who had backed him so wholeheartedly all these years would rally behind his choice as well. Pandian, too, seemed to have had little inkling of the groundswell of antipathy building up against him. That someone – an unelected outsider – was wielding so much power and was now positioned to succeed Naveen in the future, hurt regional sentiments and local sensibilities. Adding to the anguish was that a non-Odia was virtually leading the BJD – a regional outfit sworn to protecting and promoting Odia identity. Pandian's preeminence at the cost of all local leaders offended local self-respect. Suddenly, the issue of Odia *Asmita* (Odia pride) took centerstage.

Pandian, though, had other plans. Back in 2019, when Naveen was re-elected and sworn in as chief minister on Pandian's birthday, he had designated Pandian as the '5T secretary'. 5T was a non-existent department. It was Naveen's initiative for better management of Teamwork, Transparency, Technology, Time and Transformation in the state, and Pandian's appointment allowed him to interfere in every other department and stamp his authority. As the elections in 2024 drew near, he launched what he considered was a charm offensive. He began to aggressively hard sell what he claimed were transformative changes (Rupantar) brought about by his boss during his long rule.

Naveen and his team never tired of publicizing what they felt were momentous achievements. A subservient media alongside huge advertising budgets helped them to ceaselessly amplify their claims. According to them, Odisha's growth rate had outpaced the national average, standing at 7.8 per cent against the national average of 7 per cent in 2022–2023. Per capita, they claimed, had grown three times since FY12, while the unemployment rate in the state was the lowest in the country – only 0.9 per cent compared to 8.3 per cent in the country. The government also claimed that it had made tremendous headway in reducing poverty, insisting that more than 6.2 million people were brought out of poverty in the past five years alone.

The claims made were tall indeed. Rice production, the government said, had grown from 0.1 metric tons in FY04 to 5.4 metric tons in FY23; land under irrigation had increased to 12.2 million acres by 2023–2024 from 6.26 million acres in 2000–2001; infant mortality had been cut down from 95 deaths per 1,000 live births in 2000 to just 36 per 1,000 live births in 2020; maternal mortality had fallen by 305 points between 1999–2001 and 2018–2020, and 21,250 new government schools (besides 22 new government universities and 10 medical colleges) had been opened in the state in the intervening years.

But to Pandian's misfortune, his 'Rupantar' campaign misfired. The lived experiences of most Odias did not match the claims of betterment. With employment being scarce, unemployment was soaring, with the *Indian Employment Report 2024* by the International Labour Organisation[1] stating that Odisha ranked the lowest among 22 major states surveyed. Tens of thousands migrated out of the state every year in search of livelihood. The state was also parched, with the state's drinking water supply coverage of 68.6 per cent in rural areas short of the national average of 71.1 per cent. Educational infrastructure was in shambles as well. Among everything else, 30 per cent of the state's 53,997 schools had no supply of potable water, only 8.1 per cent of government schools had internet, 81.7 per cent of government schools had no computers, and some 48.2 per cent of the government secondary schools had no integrated science laboratories. More worryingly, 9,510 of rural schools had no electricity, 21,179 schools were without playgrounds, and almost 20 per cent of teacher posts in government high

---

[1] Available at http://www.indiaenvironmentportal.org.in/files/file/India%20Employment%20Report%202024.pdf

schools were vacant. To top it all, in Odisha's schools, the dropout rate in class 10 was the highest in the country – standing at a whopping 49.9 per cent.

It is no wonder that Pandian's push to impress the electorate failed to cut much ice, just as his audacious efforts to win over the BJP – the principal opposition in the state – to the BJD's side came a cropper as well. It is unbelievable that a ruling party could be batting alongside the opposition in any state. But what was incredible elsewhere was an ordinary reality for Odisha with the ruling party and the principal opposition working together clandestinely, almost as allies. Unlike in neighbouring West Bengal, where the BJP persisted with its noisy offensive against Mamata Banerjee's Trinamool Congress, the party was comparatively muted in Odisha. The BJD reciprocated in adequate measure, voting in Parliament in favour of the ruling NDA almost on all issues – from opposing the no-confidence motion against Prime Minister Modi to supporting the Centre's legislation to strip the Delhi government of all authority. That a regional party sworn to strengthening federalism could facilitate the dismantling of the powers of a popularly elected state government was difficult to digest. But smug in the belief that it was beyond reproach, the BJD continued to do the unthinkable with only its self-interest in mind. BJD ministers faced no CBI or ED heat either.

With just months left for the general elections, efforts were made to strengthen the ties. In early 2024, when a few Rajya Sabha seats from Odisha fell vacant, the BJD promptly sent several of its chosen candidates to the Upper House. Interestingly though, it did not put up a candidate for one seat. And when the BJP chose union railways minister Ashwini Vaishnaw to contest from the seat, the BJD threw its weight behind him, saying it would support the minister's candidature. The BJP did not have the requisite numbers in the assembly to get Vaishnaw elected. But with the BJD backing him – ostensibly to carry forward the laudable expansion of rail networks across the state – Vaishnaw romped home, and the bond between the BJP and BJD reached a new level altogether.

Pandian, in hindsight, had little political acumen despite having come to wield immense power. Some senior BJD leaders, in fact, preferred to describe him behind closed doors as an 'intelligent fool'. Lulled by the BJD's close association with the BJP, Pandian lost sight of the time-tested proverb that there are no permanent friends or enemies in politics. While he attempted to stitch a formal alliance ('menta' in Odia) with the BJP for the purposes of fighting the impending elections together, state BJP leaders silently nursed other plans.

If Pandian had succeeded in pulling off a formal alliance with the BJP, it would have been a masterstroke. Besides being the principal opposition party, the BJP was resourceful; it had the bandwidth to turn the tide against Pandian by aggressively exploiting his outsider status and stoking the issue of Odia Asmita. Pandian calculated that the BJP could be silenced if brought over to BJD's side. His plans to succeed Naveen would also become smooth.

Aided by a grateful Vaishnaw and another influential official in the PMO hailing from Odisha, BJD's push for an electoral alliance with the BJP almost came to fruition. Pandian made several secretive visits to Delhi on a chartered plane and held midnight parleys. Words spread that an alliance brokered in New Delhi was on the cards, and a shadow of grief enveloped the state BJP headquarters. State BJP leaders had, for long, helplessly watched the closeness of the BJD with their central leaders. Their voices mattered little as the NDA government – short of numbers in the Rajya Sabha – actively sought Naveen's assistance to navigate troubled times. But to meekly surrender again and side with the BJD in state elections was too much of a bitter pill to swallow and the state leaders put their collective foot down. They simply could not bring themselves around to support an alliance with the ruling party that would allow the Congress to revive by default and occupy the opposition space in the state once again. By then, many of them also had a fair idea about the public antipathy growing over Pandian's meteoric rise. They used all their might and finally succeeded in bringing the central leadership back to their senses. The alliance was finally off, and Pandian's plan came to nought.

But Naveen's erstwhile secretary and potential successor was not done yet. Comforted by the party's success in 2019 elections and then again in the panchayat elections in Odisha in 2022, he believed in the party's 'bright' electoral prospects. In 2019, too, as during the 2024 campaign, the BJP had threatened to dump the BJD into the Bay of Bengal. 'The BJD government is a burnt transformer,'[2] union home minister Amit Shah had famously thundered before the 2019 polls, claiming that they would win no less than 120 assembly seats and throw the ruling party out. But if a tsunami in favour of the BJP was promised, it did not result even in a single ripple. Naveen rode back to power, winning some 112 of the 147 seats. The BJP came a distant second, securing just 23 seats. The same occurred with the state-wide panchayat elections held in 2022. Having done

---

[2] Available at https://www.business-standard.com/article/news-ians/shah-equates-bjd-govt-with-burnt-transformer-119020300574_1.html

creditably well in the previous polls of 2017 – when it won 297 Zilla Parishad seats compared to its earlier tally of 36 – the BJP's tally in 2022 plummeted again. Naveen's BJD won 766 of 852 Zilla Parishads while the BJP had to be content with only 42.

Convinced that Odisha remained Naveen's unchallenged fiefdom, Pandian thought he would reap huge electoral dividends. With election dates announced and candidates chosen, the BJD announced a list of 40 star-campaigners who would canvass votes for the party. It included senior leaders and a smattering of Odia cinema stars. But when the campaign started, it was Pandian and Pandian alone who occupied the spotlight. Naveen made guest appearances – doing a roadshow here and an odd rally there. But it was mostly Pandian all the way. No other star campaigners were seen during the campaign as Pandian, drenched in sweat and still in his customary tight trousers and full-sleeves shirt, strode from one rally site to another. When not addressing crowds, he staged road shows from atop a refurbished van to wave at bewildered passersby. The former bureaucrat, in fact, held road shows the very same evening in towns and cities across the state where Prime Minister Modi had campaigned earlier during the day.

While the BJD and the BJP went head-to-head, the Congress was missing from the frenetic electioneering altogether. Having ruled Odisha for very long spells until early 2000, the grand old party now stands obscured from plain sight. To say that the party risks extinction would be no exaggeration. The BJP's rise in the state has come largely at its cost. And nowhere is the party's despondency on better display than at its organizational headquarters in the heart of Bhubaneswar – opposite the railway station and on the spacious road leading to the state assembly and the secretariat along which Republic Day and Independence Day parades take place. That stretch of road is also the favourite destination for protesters from all over the state, who gather there almost every day to air their grievances on some issue or another. Sitting amid the din and bustle, the Congress office, located within a spacious compound, is mostly quiet and deserted. The sight that greets one there is of a motley group of men lounging around on plastic chairs in the lobby, chewing paan and doing precious little. Rows of offices remain locked, bearing silent testimony to the fact that the party in the state is well past its prime.

Since being voted out of power in Odisha in 2000, it has been a downhill journey for the party that once enjoyed considerable sway over a sizeable section of the people, particularly in its poor tribal belts. The Congress's domination was never total, though, and it often had to lean on regional parties to form government in the past. But in regions such as Koraput and Nowrangpur, inhabitants worshipped Jawaharlal Nehru and Indira Gandhi to such an extent that only Congress candidates won parliamentary contests from there. Gamang, Odisha's chief minister when the super cyclone struck in 1999, was elected to the Lok Sabha from Koraput no less than nine times – in 1972, 1977, 1980, 1984, 1989, 1991, 1996, 1998 and 2004. Khagapati Pradhani also won nine times from Nowrangpur – in 1967, 1971, 1977, 1980, 1984, 1989, 1991, 1996 and 1998. However, the party's heydays are long gone. But for Koraput – a parliamentary seat that it won both in 2019 and 2024 – it has ceded ground to other parties everywhere else.

The tragedies that have befallen the Congress in Odisha are many. Its decline as a hegemonic party at the national level has been accompanied by a growing bankruptcy of ideas and leaders at the state level. Former chief minister, J.B. Patnaik, who dominated Congress politics in Odisha for decades, had little acceptance among ordinary people but enjoyed a high standing among his partymen. Other leaders who came up following Patnaik's death in 2015 had little acceptance among both people and partymen. 'Our current crop of leaders is both faceless and baseless,' scoffed a party worker from Berhampur in Ganjam. The party does try to change office-bearers as well as nominating a new president from time to time to infuse fresh blood and reinvigorate itself. But no one has made any difference to the party's fortunes.

The procession of presidents has not taken the party anywhere. If anything, the game of musical chairs has heightened factionalism within the party. Each one of the presidents promised a better future and insisted that the Congress was a bit down but not out. But plagued by the lack of a credible and popular face, the party is rudderless. Its showing in the elections never lived up to what it's presidents predicted.

The party's vote share in Odisha has shrunk alarmingly. In 2000, when it was voted out in favour of Naveen Patnaik's BJD, the Congress had 33.78 per cent of the votes, winning 26 of the 147 assembly seats. In 2004, it did marginally better, winning 34.82 per cent of the votes with 38 seats. But in 2009, the Congress got only 29.1 per cent of the votes and won just 27 seats. In 2014, its vote share shrank further to 25.7 per cent and it got only 16 assembly seats. In 2019, this was down to 16.3 per cent with just 9 seats.

From 2009, hapless Congressmen began deserting the party to join the BJD in search of greener pastures.

Before the 2014 elections, Bhupinder Singh, the leader of the Congress legislative party, switched sides and went over to the BJD. The high-profile defection drained the party's morale before even a single vote had been cast in the elections.

It is not that the central leadership of the party has not tried to revive the party's fortunes in the state. Rahul Gandhi has visited Odisha several times – just as he did during the 2024 election campaign – but he has not been embraced by any group in the entire state. Each time he tours the state, Gandhi addresses rallies but leaves no lasting impression.

The panchayat polls of 2017 reconfirmed the rapid slide of the Congress in the state. The party managed to secure an embarrassing 18.04 per cent of the votes and was relegated to the third spot by the BJP, which won 33.03 per cent of the votes against the BJD's 40.81 per cent. Congressmen in Odisha were already leaving the party in droves for the BJD. Now, many began to leave for the BJP as well.

'If one has to do politics in Odisha, one has to be either with the BJD or the BJP. Being with the Congress is committing political suicide,' admitted a Congress partyman who had contested the 2014 elections and come a distant third. Earlier, the BJD was the preferred destination for party deserters. However, hundreds are leaving for the BJP since 2014.

Lalatendu Bidhyadhar Mohapatra, who died in 2016, was an influential Congress leader and a former legislator, popular among the younger rank and file of the party. A year later, his daughter Upasna Mohapatra, together with hundreds of loyalists, joined the BJP. Politics, after all, is about gaining power. Many Congress partymen, therefore, are choosing to align themselves with political parties that promise better electoral dividends.

Things worked out well for Upasna after she ditched her father's party and chose the BJP. In 2024, she won her first election to the state assembly from her family borough of Brahmagiri in Puri district. At most places, Congress candidates lost. When the 2024 election results came out, the Congress cut a sorry figure. It won just 14 of the state's assembly seats and only one of Odisha's 21 parliamentary seats. Among the losers were its top leaders – Sarat Patnaik, Niranjan Patnaik and Jaydev Jena. Sarat Patnaik, who led the party in the latest election battle, in fact, lost his deposit. That diehard Congressmen hoping for a Congress revival were only daydreaming was evident the evening when Bhakta Charan Das – a former union minister and chief of the Congress campaign committee in Odisha – sat alone in his room in a Bhubaneswar hotel in the midst of peak electioneering. He had no men or money and no means to make an impact. Unlike in Telangana, where an out-of-favour Congress surprised everyone by storming back to power in recent months under the charismatic leadership of A. Revanth Reddy, the Congress in Odisha faced a more daunting task. In Telangana, in the worst of times, the Congress vote share had not dropped below 35 per cent. In Odisha, it was down to some 16 per cent. To pull the party out of such a deepening hole was too tall a task, and the Congress in Odisha failed miserably.

Currently, Congressmen in the state are simply trudging along. Some of them are incurable loyalists, such as Subhash Chandra Samatasinghar of Nimapada in Puri district. '*Hatha thiley bhata khaiba* (I will eat only if I have a hand)', said Samatasinghar, referring to the Congress symbol to convey his undying loyalty to the party. There are also a few who will not be accepted into their fold either by the BJD or the BJP, and are therefore in the Congress. The party for the Congress has well and truly been over in Odisha for quite some time.

The BJD finds itself in similar despair post the 2024-polls. Though Naveen Patnaik remains popular, Pandian was an unmitigated disaster. The more he stomped across Odisha to canvas for his party and cement his authority as the single-most important leader after the party supremo, the more the BJD attracted public anger. Pandian, in effect, turned out to be the BJP's star campaigner – his unpopularity dwarfing Naveen's popularity.

There were other unintended consequences, too, as Pandian monopolized the party campaign. Over the years, Naveen's trusted aide had come to grab the most decision-making authority within the party. It meant other prominent leaders within the party had been sidelined. Only Pandian mattered. He had proven his worth as a backroom manager during previous polls in 2019, pulling the strings and micro-managing things from behind the scenes despite being an IAS officer. But as he hit the ground in 2024, there was no one left to run the party's central control room. Party candidates from the state's interiors made frantic bids to relay real-time feedback on the changing ground realities – from the urgent need for money to changes in popular sentiment at the local level. They required urgent remedial measures, but there was no one to act upon them with Pandian busy campaigning himself. He had left behind his own trusted team in Bhubaneshwar to tackle developing situations, but its members proved totally inept. An IPS officer close to Pandian, who reportedly also doubled up as a party agent, kept himself busy by using his police network to conduct his own surveys. His projections that the BJD would win no less than 110 of the total 147 assembly seats were proven way off the mark. When the votes were counted on 4 June, Naveen's BJD got a sound drubbing and the high-flying Pandian came crashing down to earth.

Contrary to the tall claims it constantly made in the run-up to the polls, the BJD won just 51 seats. The BJP, on the contrary, won 78 – allowing it to form the government in the state for the first time. The victory marked a momentous turning point for the BJP in Odisha. The party had been eyeing the state without much luck for long. Though backed by an elaborate RSS network that ran schools and temple management committees – touching the lives of tens of thousands across the state – the going for the BJP had proven to be tough. For one, its Hindutva agenda did not strike an instant chord with the people of Odisha. Muslims accounted for only a miniscule percentage of the population, that too in certain localized pockets such as Bhadrak, Balasore and Cuttack, and it proved difficult for the BJP to stir the people as it did elsewhere with its rabble-rousing slogans such as '*Hindu khatrein mein hain* (Hindus are in danger)'. Even the resurrection of Lord Ram and the reconstruction of the Ram temple in Ayodhya made little or no difference with Lord Jagannath undisputedly occupying a higher pedestal in the state.

The BJP desperately wished to conquer Odisha, to expand the party's footprints to newer frontiers beyond its strongholds in northern India. It made perfect sense to acquire newer areas to offset possible losses of seats in its areas of strength. The results in 2024 in Uttar Pradesh, where the BJP's Lok Sabha tally came down drastically from 62 to 33 seats, was a proof of the importance of the BJP's expansion plan. However, the party's plans have yielded only mixed results so far. The southern states have proven to be tough to crack, and the east too – states such as West Bengal – has not really yielded.

The 2024 results in Odisha should therefore give the BJP central leadership a lot to cheer. Wresting power in the state and winning 20 of the 21 Lok Sabha seats have certainly been a gamechanger. Imagine the consequences if Odisha had not given the party these many seats. With a winning tally of just 240 and short of the majority figure in Lok Sabha by 32 seats, Prime Minister Modi would have been more dependent to run his NDA government on coalition partners. The central government's future would have been more tenuous.

But then, Odisha threw up a surprise – the unthinkable happened. Naveen finally stumbled and was swept aside. In great measure, it was Pandian who helped the BJP in cutting his boss down to size. Now firmly in the saddle in the state, it was time for the BJP to have the last laugh.

6

What Next?

In the immediate aftermath of the poll drubbing, Naveen Patnaik's demeanour changed remarkably. Unlike in the recent past when he walked slowly and spoke haltingly, he suddenly had a spring in his step. Without any assistance, he climbed up the stairs of the stage for the oath-taking ceremony of the new chief minister at the Janata Maidan of Bhubaneswar a few days after the results. He then smilingly exchanged pleasantries with dignitaries present, including the prime minister. With the niceties over, Naveen went back to holding regular meetings at the sprawling Naveen Niwas with partymen – both elected and non-elected. He also periodically met up with the local press, giving them short statements on the latest developments within the BJD. And for a change, he held the microphone in his own hands – something that Odias had grown accustomed to seeing his trusted lieutenant V.K. Pandian holding for him till very recently.

Naveen's cheery transformation triggered a fresh round of speculation over the state of his health. Was he really ailing, as many had thought? Why did he look so frail and unsteady earlier? How did he suddenly regain his vigour? The mystery lingers.

Perhaps he is distraught in private and puts on a game face, appearing gung-ho about his changed circumstances in public? Naveen is now just the leader of the opposition in the Odisha assembly, and the police have been quick to dismantle the layers of barricades around his home and disappear. Security has become a lot lighter, and on the odd occasion Naveen ventures out – as he did to attend the oath-taking ceremony – he has no blaring police pilot vehicles clearing the way. In fact, even on his way home from the oath-taking ceremony, he had gotten caught in a traffic jam and made the best of the situation by repeatedly folding his hands to reciprocate the greetings of other stranded motorists.

Despite being voted out, the goodwill for Naveen has certainly not dried up. He remains popular and is by far the tallest political leader in the state. Few can match his stature. The new Odisha chief minister Mohan Charan Majhi – a four-time MLA from Keonjhar district who first started his political journey years ago as a *sarpanch* – will find it difficult to get anywhere close to the records set by his immediate predecessor.

Post 2024, the worst fall has, however, been for Pandian. Now pilloried as a villain even by the BJD men and women who used to fawn over him earlier, a contrite Pandian announced his decision to withdraw from 'active' politics through a video message. Whether he will continue to be involved in the BJD's backroom, aiding and advising his boss, remains a subject of conjecture. But for the moment, only a few in Odisha are missing Pandian. No tears were shed over his vanishing act, as abrupt as his emergence in the first place.

Naveen's BJD, though, is far from being entirely banished from the state. Despite the defeat, the party still has deep roots and controls many of the levers of power at the local level. Having resoundingly won the local body polls in 2022, the party continues to control 765 of Odisha's 852 Zilla Parishads, besides a humungous number of panchayats. It is also in power in 95 of the state's 106 civic bodies and three municipal corporations, namely Bhubaneswar, Cuttack and Berhampur. With the next round of local elections due only in 2027 – two years prior to the Lok Sabha and state assembly polls in 2029 – the BJD can certainly hope to plot a political comeback.

The party should be buoyed by the fact that it does not lack money and men. Unlike the time when Naveen's father Biju Patnaik lost power in the state in

1995 and left to become an MP in Delhi, leaving his state party unit with almost empty coffers, Naveen's BJD has pots of cash. In the six years of electoral bonds, the BJD received around Rs 944 crores – one of the highest amounts received by any regional party. Considering that there are other sources for a political party to enrich itself – cash donations being one major source – the BJD is far from being a pauper. That it boasts of one crore members should also give the BJD a lot of comfort.

Its biggest political capital, however, remains Naveen's undying popularity. The endearing goodwill for him was on show even the day the 2024 results came out. While boisterous BJP supporters celebrated their victory – in front of the party's office in Bhubaneswar – a tinge of sadness settled over other parts of the state capital. Even many who had voted against the ruling BJD, shook their heads in silent despair. 'It is sad to see a gentle Naveen go,' lamented Swapna Khuntia, a resident of an apartment on Vivekananda Marg in the old part of the city. 'He definitely deserved a more dignified send off,' added her neighbour, Rukmini Sahoo.

The disappointment over his loss is widely held, so much so that Naveen's popular standing may have gone up a notch since his defeat. The sense of loss stings harder since the 78-year-old former chief minister may not have a realistic chance to ever stage a return. Though the BJP wrested power from him, winning just four more seats than the 74 required to cross the majority mark in the assembly, its government is expected to be stable and prospects of a mid-term poll are generally ruled out. It means that the next chance Naveen would get at becoming chief minister would be in 2029. But he would be 83 years old then and could find the dice loaded against him.

To have an octogenarian assuming the office of chief minister in India is rare, though not entirely unheard of. In more recent times, V.S. Achuthanandan became chief minister of Kerala when he was 81 years old. Will Naveen be able to repeat such a feat? It is impossible to guess.

The biggest uncertainty staring the BJD in the face is over its leadership. As long as Naveen is around, he will steer the ship. It is probable that he will be able to lead the party during the 2027 panchayat elections. But few are certain what will happen thereafter, if Naveen were to exit the political stage – voluntarily or involuntarily. The vacuum he would leave would be as huge as it was in the case of his father Biju Patnaik. Of course, there are people who say that Naveen isn't in the same league as the senior Patnaik. Biju Babu was a statesman who was extremely charismatic. On the contrary, reclusive and reticent, Naveen has only mastered the art of staying in power. Though he has mass appeal, he may not have captured the people's imagination to the degree his legendary father had. In addition, Naveen, unlike his father, has never been in the opposition before or spent time in political wilderness. Even when out of power, the elder Patnaik had clout and enjoyed the unflinching loyalty of his supporters, who moved with their leader from one party to another. The same cannot be said for Naveen. True, crowds gathered around him. But how much of the crowd was because of personal devotion to him and how much was there just to reap the benefits of the power that he held for nearly a quarter of a century?

Naveen will certainly be remembered for being Odisha's longest-serving chief minister. But could the same be said about his achievements? The jury is out and opinion is largely divided. While almost everyone gives him credit for giving the state political stability, there are contrasting views on his real achievements. He gave the state some feel-good moments, such as when Odisha sponsored the Indian hockey team and hosted the hockey World Cup. He also did make the state disaster-resistant and better prepared for calamitous events such as cyclones. But when it came to addressing more substantive issues such as securing livelihoods, he was less sure-footed. The runaway rate of unemployment, the worsening water crisis and rampant outward migration, among many other things, have blighted his long rule.

All this and more makes the BJD's future uncertain. In the event of Naveen – the glue – bowing out, will the party be able to survive? Or will it disintegrate? Or will the BJP, given its present might and resources, swallow it? The present political situation is pregnant with possibilities for the future. Many things could happen, just as it did in Tamil Nadu following J. Jayalalithaa's demise. Like her AIADMK, the BJD, too, has suffered from a terrible lack of internal democracy and no other party leader has ever been allowed to grow in stature. Naveen, like Jayalalithaa, has surrounded himself with partymen who could at best be described as political pygmies. The few who showed promise of becoming big were summarily cut to size.

Given the similarities, there is every possibility that a post-Naveen scenario could resemble the post-Jayalalithaa situation that played out in Tamil Nadu. Driven by their survival instincts, partymen could elect someone non-controversial among them to succeed Naveen. Since the chosen individual may not have the same standing or the necessary acumen to carry everyone alone, chances are that the partymen will bicker and split. After all, the BJP in power in the state will find a rudderless BJD to be easy prey that can be poached, split and swallowed.

There is also the possibility that some politicians could come together to initiate another regional experiment. If the BJD – minus Naveen – is to lose steam, and if the BJP is to assert itself, there could always be a section of local leaders who will try to carve out a niche for themselves in the changing situation. A new regional party with a new face and a new slogan could just click as an alternative to the BJP.

Politics is never shorn of surprises. Who, after all, could have thought that a greenhorn like Naveen, who had nothing to do with politics for the first 52 years of his life, would scale the political heights that he finally did? But then, an Odisha adrift on helplessness, was desperate for a saviour and the non-Odia speaking Naveen came at the perfect time. One must say that luck also played an important role in helping Naveen rule the state – the first province to be carved out on linguistic lines way back in 1936. From time to time, political opponents derided him for not speaking the local language, but it ended there and went no further. A law enacted by an earlier Congress government in the 1950s stipulated that all government business must be transacted in Odia. But the law stipulated no punitive measures for anyone not complying with the provision, and in its absence, no one really bothered to follow what was laid down in the law. Naveen's administration didn't either.

Fortunately for Naveen, the importance of the local language had also diminished considerably since the time of the creation of Odisha. The state's large ST population does not necessarily speak Odia. They have their own tribal languages and converse in Odia only when required to communicate with outsiders. There is also no common version of Odia which is spoken across the state and dialects differ from region to region. The language is also believed to have failed to develop as a vehicle for imparting modern-day knowledge. Priorities have changed, and jobs and services are on top of everyone's mind. Odias remain a proud people, but Odia has slipped in their priority list and has ceased to evoke the chauvinism that Tamil or Marathi do among their speakers. Language not being an emotive issue in Odisha allowed Naveen to establish himself there, where, according to a 1994 law, written and spoken knowledge of Odia is a must for contesting gram panchayat elections. It was Naveen's luck that knowledge of the local language wasn't mandatory for the state's highest elected position. Though unqualified to be a lowly gram panchayat member, he was eligible to serve as the chief minister.

Perhaps, destiny also played a part in taking Naveen so far. At least, so believed a renowned astrologer from Paralakhemundi of Odisha's southern Gajapati district. Soon after Naveen had taken over as chief minister in 2000, the astrologer, now dead, had been called over by some of Naveen's aides to pore over his horoscope and help with information about what the future portended. The astrologer made several predictions, including Naveen winning all elections between 2000 and 2019. Not a great believer in what the stars foretell, Naveen heard the prediction but never reacted. It's a different matter that the astrologer was proven correct again and again. Naveen won re-elections in 2004, 2009, 2014 and 2019.

But how did the astrologer know, way back in 2000, that there would be elections in 2019? Assembly elections are normally held every five years. Going by that, Odisha ought to have had elections in 2020. But Naveen had unexpectedly advanced the 2005 elections to 2004, and that brought forward all the subsequent assembly elections by a year.

The astrologer stopped predicting Naveen's political future after predicting his victory in 2019. He did make one other personal prediction, but never attempted at guessing what would happen in the elections after 2019. As it turned out, Naveen lost in 2024, losing his sheen as an 'unbeaten' politician. It dented his record a bit, but did precious little to harm his standing as a political phenomenon.

Naveen Patnaik, the politician, will be hard to match, after all.

Acknowledgements

This book is a collective labour of love. Many others were committed and deeply invested in the book, and they included Chiki Sarkar, Parth Mehrotra and Rhea Gupta of Juggernaut Books.

While I am grateful to Chiki for being a wonderful publisher, I am grateful to Parth for stoically bearing with me as I badgered him periodically over the years for an updated version of the book. He advised me to be patient. His sense of timing turned out to be perfect, as this revised and updated version comes out possibly at the right time – post the 2024 elections.

Rhea's thoughtful edits of the manuscript helped in great measure. She deserves much of the credit for the book.

I am also grateful to many others, including the many senior bureaucrats who spoke at length and helped me with insights into the personality of Naveen Patnaik. Their contribution was immense. Some retired, some still in service, I have deliberately refrained from naming any of them to protect their confidentiality. But they would know who they are, and I am extremely grateful to each of them.

I am also thankful to my many friends in Bhubaneswar who helped in very many ways. My young journalist friend Debabrata Mohanty deserves a special mention. He did not complain even once as I constantly asked him to run around to get data and details.

Finally, I must acknowledge the contribution of my family: my wife Amrita, daughter Rupsa and son-in-law Umang. All three kept my morale up even when the chips were evidently down.

Index

Index

A Note on the Author

Ruben Banerjee, former group editor-in-chief of *Outlook*, is a veteran journalist who has worked with *Hindustan Times*, *Al Jazeera*, *India Today* and *Indian Express*. Currently the general secretary of the Editors Guild of India, he is also the author of the books – *The Odisha Tragedy: A Cyclone's Year of Calamity* and *Editor Missing: The Media in Today's India*.